Encyclopaedia of Banking and Finance

Encyclopaedia of Banking and Finance

Hemant Sharma

CYBER TECH PUBLICATIONS
4264/3, Ansari Road, Daryaganj, New Delhi-110002 (India)
Ph.: 011-23244078. Fax: 011-23280028
E-Mail: cyberpublicationsdelhi@yahoo.com

ENCYCLOPAEDIA OF BANKING AND FINANCE

Hemant Sharma

First Edition 2009

Published by :

G.S. Rawat for **Cyber Tech Publications**
4264/3, Ansari Road, Daryaganj, New Delhi-110002 (India)
Ph.: 011-23244078. Fax: 011-23280028
E-Mail: cyberpublicationsdelhi@yahoo.com

Printed at : **Amit Enterprises**, Maujpur, Delhi, (9810878184)

Preface

This book is designed to help the reader understand the environment and modus operandi of multinational banks, with the focus on policy- and concept-oriented issues in the arena of international banking. It fills what I feel is a pressing need in international business curricula. Each chapter addresses the theory and practice of international banking. The contents are suitable for the practitioner as well as M.B.A. and advanced undergraduate students. How ever, a basic knowledge of international finance and economics is presumed. The subject's broad scope adds interest but creates problems. There is a long menu of topics that may be included in a book of this nature. The difficulty of selecting what to include is especially acute for professors who are structuring college-level courses in international banking. This volume takes an approach that is both narrow and broad--the former in the sense of focusing only on important macro-policy issues and key international concepts, the latter in the sense of covering about twelve major subject areas. One final comment on content should be mentioned. Most books dealing with contemporary issues are vulnerable to the possibility of events overtaking them. Today's issues become tomorrow's history. An attempt is made to reduce this problem by including selections of topics that are relatively timeless.

This book owes much to many people. Any deficiencies in style or sub stance are the sole responsibility of the author.

—Author

CONTENTS

1

BANK: AN INTRODUCTION

A banker or bank is a financial institution that acts as a payment agent for customers, and borrows and lends money. In some countries such as Germany and Japan banks are the primary owners of industrial corporations while in other countries such as the United States banks are prohibited from owning non-financial companies.

The first modern bank was founded in Italy at Genoa in 1406, its name was "Banco di San Giorgio" (Bank of St. George).

Banks act as payment agents by conducting checking or current accounts for customers, paying cheques drawn by customers on the bank, and collecting cheques deposited to customers' current accounts. Banks also enable customer payments via other payment methods such as telegraphic transfer, EFTPOS, and ATM.

Banks borrow money by accepting funds deposited on current account, accepting term deposits and by issuing debt securities such as banknotes and bonds. Banks lend money by making advances to customers on current account, by making installment loans, and by investing in marketable debt securities and other forms of lending.

Banks provide almost all payment services, and a bank account is considered indispensable by most businesses, individuals and governments. Non-banks that provide payment services such as remittance companies are not normally considered an adequate substitute for having a bank account.

Banks borrow most funds borrowed from households and non-financial businesses, and lend most funds lent to households and non-financial businesses, but non-bank lenders provide a significant and in many cases adequate substitute for bank loans, and money market funds, cash management trusts and other non-bank financial institutions in many cases provide an adequate substitute to banks for lending savings to.

DEFINITION OF A BANK

The definition of a bank varies from country to country.

Under English law, a bank is defined as a person who carries on the business of banking, which is specified as:

- conducting current accounts for customers
- paying cheques drawn on a given person, and
- collecting cheques for their customers.

In most English common law jurisdictions there is a Bills of Exchange Act that codifies the law in relation to negotiable instruments, including cheques, and this Act contains a statutory definition of the term banker : ' banker includes a body of persons, whether incorporated or not, who carry on the business of banking' (Section 2, Interpretation). Although this definition seems circular, it is actually functional, because it ensures that the legal basis for bank transactions such as cheques do not depend on how the bank is organised or regulated.

The business of banking is in many English common law countries not defined by statute but by common law, the definition above. In other English common law jurisdictions there are statutory definitions of the business of banking or banking business.

When looking at these definitions it is important to keep in mind that they are defining the business of banking for the purposes of the legislation, and not necessarily in general. In particular, most of the definitions are from legislation that has the purposes of entry regulating and supervising banks rather than regulating the actual business of banking. However, in many cases the statutory definition closely mirrors the common law one. Examples of statutory definitions:

- "banking business" means the business of receiving money on current or deposit account, paying and collecting cheques drawn by or paid in by customers, the making of advances to customers, and includes such other business as the Authority may prescribe for the purposes of this Act;' (Banking Act (Singapore), Section 2, Interpretation).
- "banking business" means the business of either or both of the following:
    1. receiving from the general public money on current, deposit, savings or other similar account repayable on demand or within less than [3 months]... or with a period of call or notice of less than that period;
    2. paying or collecting cheques drawn by or paid in by customers; (Banking Ordinance, Section 2, Interpretation, Hong Kong) Note that in this case the definition is extended to include accepting any deposits repayable in less than 3 months, companies that accept deposits of greater than HK$100 000 for periods of greater than 3 months are regulated as deposit taking companies rather than as banks in Hong Kong).

Since the advent of EFTPOS (Electronic Funds Transfer at Point Of Sale), direct credit, direct debit and internet banking, the cheque has lost its primacy in most banking systems as a payment instrument.

This has lead legal theorists to suggest that the cheque based definition should be broadened to include financial institutions that conduct current accounts for customers and enable customers to pay and be paid by third parties, even if they do not pay and collect cheques.

Wider Commercial Role of Banks

However the commercial role of banks is wider than banking, and includes:

- issue of banknotes (promissory notes issued by a banker and payable to bearer on demand)
- processing of payments by way of telegraphic transfer, EFTPOS, internet banking or other means
- issuing bank drafts and bank cheques
- accepting money on term deposit
- lending money by way of overdraft, installment loan or otherwise
- providing documentary and standby letters of credit, guarantees, performance bonds, securities underwriting commitments and other forms of off balance sheet exposures
- safekeeping of documents and other items in safe deposit boxes
- currency exchange
- sale, distribution or brokerage, with or without advice, of insurance, unit trusts and similar financial products as a 'financial supermarket'

Economic Functions

The economic functions of banks include:

1. issue of money, in the form of banknotes and current accounts subject to cheque or payment at the customer's order. These claims on banks can act as money because they are negotiable and/or repayable on demand, and hence valued at par and effectively transferable by mere delivery in the case of banknotes, or by drawing a cheque, delivering it to the payee to bank or cash.
2. netting and settlement of payments--banks act both as collection agent and paying agents for customers, and participate in inter-bank clearing and settlement systems to collect, present, be presented with, and pay payment instruments. This enables banks to economise on reserves held for settlement of payments, since inward and outward payments offset each other. It also enables payment flows between geographical arcas to offset, reducing the cost of settling payments between geographical areas.
3. credit intermediation--banks borrow and lend back-to-back on their own account as middle men
4. credit quality improvement--banks lend money to ordinary commercial and personal borrowers (ordinary credit quality), but are high quality borrowers. The improvement comes from diversification of the bank's assets and the bank's own capital which provides a buffer to absorb losses without defaulting on its own obligations. However, since banknotes and deposits are generally unsecured, if the bank gets into difficulty and pledges assets as security to try to get the funding it needs to continue to operate, this puts the note holders and depositors in an economically subordinated position.

5. maturity transformation--banks borrow more on demand debt and short term debt, but provide more long term loans. Bank can do this because they can aggregate issues (e.g. accepting deposits and issuing banknotes) and redemptions (e.g. withdrawals and redemptions of banknotes), maintain reserves of cash, invest in marketable securities that can be readily converted to cash if needed, and raise replacement funding as needed from various sources (e.g. wholesale cash markets and securities markets) because they have a high and more well known credit quality than most other borrowers.

LAW OF BANKING

Banking law is based on a contractual analysis of the relationship between the bank and the customer. The definition of bank is given above, and the definition of customer is any person for whom the bank agrees to conduct an account.

The law implies rights and obligations into this relationship as follows:

1. The bank account balance is the financial position between the bank and the customer, when the account is in credit, the bank owes the balance to the customer, when the account is overdrawn, the customer owes the balance to the bank.
2. The bank engages to pay the customer's cheques up to the amount standing to the credit of the customer's account, plus any agreed overdraft limit.
3. The bank may not pay from the customer's account without a mandate from the customer, e.g. a cheque drawn by the customer.
4. The bank engages to promptly collect the cheques deposited to the customer's account as the customer's

agent, and to credit the proceeds to the customer's account.

5. The bank has a right to combine the customer's accounts, since each account is just an aspect of the same credit relationship.
6. The bank has a lien on cheques deposited to the customer's account, to the extent that the customer is indebted to the bank.
7. The bank must not disclose the details of the transactions going through the customer's account unless the customer consents, there is a public duty to disclose, the bank's interests require it, or under compulsion of law.
8. The bank must not close a customer's account without reasonable notice to the customer, because cheques are outstanding in the ordinary course of business for several days.

These implied contractual terms may be modified by express agreement between the customer and the bank. The statutes and regulations in force in the jurisdiction may also modify the above terms and/or create new rights, obligations or limitations relevant to the bank-customer relationship.

ENTRY REGULATION

Currently in most jurisdictions commercial banks are regulated and require a bank licence to operate.

Usually the definition of the business of banking for the purposes of regulation is extended to include acceptance of deposits, even if they are not repayable to the customer's order, however money lending, by itself, is generally not included in the definition. Unlike most other regulated industries, the regulator is typically also a participant in the market, i.e. government owned bank (a central bank). Central banks also typically have a monopoly on the business of issuing banknotes. However, in some countries this is not the case, e.g. in the UK the Financial Services Authority licences banks and some commercial banks, such as the Bank of Scotland, issue their own banknotes in competition with the Bank of England, the UK government's central bank.

Some types of entity may be partly or wholly exempt from bank licence requirements and are regulated by separate regulators, e.g. building societies and credit unions.

The requirements for the issue of a bank licence vary between juristictions but typically incude:

1. Minimum capital
2. Minimum capital ratio
3. 'Fit and Proper' requirements for the bank's controllers, owners, directors, and/or senior officers
4. Approval of the bank's business plan as being sufficiently prudent and plausible.

POLITICS AND HISTORY

Banks have influenced economies and politics for centuries. Historically, the primary purpose of a bank was to provide loans to trading companies. Banks provided funds to allow businesses to purchase inventory, and collected those funds back with interest when the goods were sold. For centuries, the banking industry only dealt with businesses, not consumers. Commercial lending today is a very intense activity, with banks carefully analysing the financial condition of their business clients to determine the level of risk in each loan transaction. Banking services have expanded to include services directed at individuals, and risk in these much smaller transactions are pooled.

ORIGIN OF THE WORD

The name bank derives from the Italian word banco "desk/bench", used during the Renaissance by Florentines bankers, who used to make their transactions above a desk covered by a green tablecloth. However, there are traces of banking activity even in ancient times. In fact, the word traces its origins back to the Ancient Roman Empire, where moneylenders would set up their stalls in the middle of enclosed courtyards called macella on a long bench called a bancu, from which the words banco and bank are derived. As a moneychanger, the merchant at the bancu did not so much invest money as merely convert the foreign currency into the only legal tender in Rome-that of the Imperial Mint.

BANKING CHANNELS

Banks offer many different channels to access their banking and other services:

- A branch, banking centre or financial centre is a retail location where a bank or financial institution offers a wide array of face to face service to its customers
- ATM is a computerised telecommunications device that provides a financial institution's customers a method of financial transactions in a public space without the need for a human clerk or bank teller. Most banks now have more ATMs than branches, and ATMs are providing a wider range of services to a wider range of users. For example in Hong Kong, most ATMs enable anyone to deposit cash to any customer of the bank's account by feeding in the notes and entering the account number to be credited. Also, most ATMs enable card holders from other banks to get their account balance and withdraw cash, even if the card is issued by a foreign bank.

- Mail is part of the postal system which itself is a system wherein written documents typically enclosed in envelopes, and also small packages containing other matter, are delivered to destinations around the world. This can be used to deposit cheques and to send orders to the bank to pay money to third parties. Banks also normally use mail to deliver periodic account statements to customers.
- Telephone banking is a service provided by a financial institution which allows its customers to perform transactions over the telephone. This normally includes bill payments for bills from major billers (e.g. for electricity).
- Online banking is a term used for performing transactions, payments etc. over the Internet through a bank, credit union or building society's secure website

TYPES OF BANKS

Banks' activities can be divided into retail banking, dealing directly with individuals and small businesses; business banking, providing services to mid-market business; corporate banking, directed at large business entities; private banking, providing wealth management services to High Net Worth Individuals and families; and investment banking, relating to activities on the financial markets. Most banks are profit-making, private enterprises. However, some are owned by government, or are non-profits.

Central banks are normally government owned banks, often charged with quasi-regulatory responsibilities, e.g. supervising commercial banks, or controlling the cash interest rate. They generally provide liquidity to the banking system and act as Lender of last resort in event of a crisis.

TYPES OF RETAIL BANKS

- Commercial bank: the term used for a normal bank to distinguish it from an investment bank. After the Great Depression, the U.S. Congress required that banks only engage in banking activities, whereas investment banks were limited to capital market activities. Since the two no longer have to be under separate ownership, some use the term "commercial bank" to refer to a bank or a division of a bank that mostly deals with deposits and loans from corporations or large businesses.
- Community Banks: locally operated financial institutions that empower employees to make local decisions to serve their customers and the partners
- Community development banks: regulated banks that provide financial services and credit to underserved markets or populations.
- Postal savings banks: savings banks associated with national postal systems.
- Private banks: manage the assets of high net worth individuals.
- Offshore banks: banks located in jurisdictions with low taxation and regulation. Many offshore banks are essentially private banks.
- Savings bank: in Europe, savings banks take their roots in the 19th or sometimes even 18th century. Their original objective was to provide easily accessible savings products to all strata of the population. In some countries, savings banks were created on public initiative, while in others socially committed individuals created foundations to put in place the necessary infrastructure. Nowadays, European savings banks have kept their focus on

retail banking: payments, savings products, credits and insurances for individuals or small and medium-sized enterprises. Apart from this retail focus, they also differ from commercial banks by their broadly decentralised distribution network, providing local and regional outreach and by their socially responsible approach to business and society.

- Building societies and Landesbanks: conduct retail banking.
- Ethical banks: banks that prioritize the transparency of all operations and make only what they consider to be socially-responsible investments.
- Islamic banks: Banks that transact according to Islamic principles.

Types of Investment Banks

- Investment banks "underwrite" (guarantee the sale of) stock and bond issues, trade for their own accounts, make markets, and advise corporations on capital markets activities such as mergers and acquisitions.
- Merchant banks were traditionally banks which engaged in trade financing. The modern definition, however, refers to banks which provide capital to firms in the form of shares rather than loans. Unlike Venture capital firms, they tend not to invest in new companies.

Both Combined

Universal banks, more commonly known as a financial services company, engage in several of these activities. For example, First Bank (a very large bank) is involved in commercial and retail lending, and its subsidiaries in tax-havens offer offshore banking services to customers in other countries. Other large financial institutions are similarly diversified and engage in multiple activities. In Europe and Asia, big banks are very diversified groups that, among other services, also distribute insurance, -hence the term bancassurance is the term used to describe the sale of insurance products in a bank. The word is a combination of "banque or bank" and "assurance" signifying that both banking and insurance are provided by the same corporate entity.

OTHER TYPES OF BANKS

Islamic Banking

Islamic banks adhere to the concepts of Islamic law. Islamic banking revolves around several well established concepts which are based on Islamic canons. Since the concept of interest is forbidden in Islam, all banking activities must avoid interest. Instead of interest, the bank earns profit (mark-up) and fees on financing facilities that it extends to the customers.

BANKS IN THE ECONOMY

Size of Global Banking Industry

Worldwide assets of the largest 1,000 banks grew 15.5% in 2005 to reach a record $60.5 trillion. This follows a 19.3% increase in the previous year. EU banks held the largest share, 50% at the end of 2005, up from 38% a decade earlier. The growth in Europe's share was mostly at the expense of Japanese banks whose share more than halved during this period from 33% to 13%. The share of US banks also rose, from 10% to 14%. Most of the remainder was from other Asian and European countries.

The US had by far the most banks (7,540 at end-2005) and branches (75,000) in the world. The large number of banks in the US is an indicator of its geography and regulatory structure, resulting in a large number of small to medium sized institutions in its banking system. Japan had 129 banks and 12,000 branches. In 2004, Germany, France, and Italy had more than 30,000 branches each-more than double the 15,000 branches in the UK.

Bank Crisis

Banks are susceptible to many forms of risk which have triggered occasional systemic crises. Risks include liquidity risk (the risk that many depositors will request withdrawals beyond available funds), credit risk (the risk that those who owe money to the bank will not repay), and interest rate risk (the risk that the bank will become unprofitable if rising interest rates force it to pay relatively more on its deposits than it receives on its loans), among others.

Banking crises have developed many times throughout history when one or more risks materialize for a banking sector as a whole. Prominent examples include the U.S. Savings and Loan crisis in 1980s and early 1990s the Japanese banking crisis during the 1990s, the bank run that occurred during the Great Depression, and the recent liquidation by the central Bank of Nigeria, where about 25 banks were liquidated.

Challenges within the Banking Industry

The banking industry is a highly regulated industry with detailed and focused regulators. All banks with FDIC-insured deposits have the FDIC as a regulator; however, for examinations, the Federal Reserve is the primary federal regulator for Fed-member state banks; the Office of the Comptroller of the Currency ("OCC") is the primary federal regulator for national banks; and the Office of Thrift Supervision, or OTS, is the primary federal regulator for thrifts. State non-member banks are examined by the state agencies as well as the FDIC. National banks have one primary regulator-the OCC.

Each regulatory agency has their own set of rules and regulations to which banks and thrifts must adhere.

The Federal Financial Institutions Examination Council (FFIEC) was established in 1979 as a formal interagency body empowered to prescribe uniform principles, standards, and report forms for the federal examination of financial institutions. Although the FFIEC has resulted in a greater degree of regulatory consistency between the agencies, the rules and regulations are constantly changing.

In addition to changing regulations, changes in the industry have led to consolidations within the Federal Reserve, FDIC, OTS and OCC. Offices have been closed, supervisory regions have been merged, staff levels have been reduced and budgets have been cut. The remaining regulators face an increased burden with increased workload and more banks per regulator. While banks struggle to keep up with the changes in the regulatory environment, regulators struggle to manage their workload and effectively regulate their banks. The impact of these changes is that banks are receiving less hands-on assessment by the regulators, less time spent with each institution, and the potential for more problems slipping through the cracks, potentially resulting in an overall increase in bank failures across the United States.

The changing economic environment has a significant impact on banks and thrifts as they struggle to effectively manage their interest rate spread in the face of low rates on loans, rate competition for deposits and the general market changes, industry trends and economic fluctuations. It has been a challenge for banks to effectively set their growth strategies with the recent economic market. A rising interest rate environment may seem to help financial institutions, but the effect of the changes on consumers and businesses is not predictable and the challenge remains for banks to grow and effectively manage the spread to generate a return to their shareholders.

The management of the banks' asset portfolios also remains a challenge in today's economic environment. Loans are a bank's primary asset category and when loan quality becomes suspect, the foundation of a bank is shaken to the core. While always an issue for banks, declining asset quality has become a big problem for financial institutions. There are several reasons for this, one of which is the lax attitude some banks have adopted because of the years of "good times."

The potential for this is exacerbated by the reduction in the regulatory oversight of banks and in some cases depth of management. Problems are more likely to go undetected, resulting in a significant impact on the bank when they are recognized. In addition, banks, like any business, struggle to cut costs and have consequently eliminated certain expenses, such as adequate employee training programs.

Banks also face a host of other challenges such as aging ownership groups. Across the country, many banks' management teams and board of directors are aging. Banks also face ongoing pressure by shareholders, both public and private, to achieve earnings and growth projections. Regulators place added pressure on banks to manage the various categories of risk. Banking is also an extremely competitive industry. Competing in the financial services industry has become tougher with the entrance of such players as insurance agencies, credit unions, check cashing services, credit card companies, etc.

Profitability

A bank generates a profit from the differential between the level of interest it pays for deposits and other sources of funds, and the level of interest it charges in its lending activities. This difference is referred to as the spread between the cost of funds and the loan interest rate. Historically, profitability from lending activities has been cyclical and dependent on the needs and strengths of loan customers. In recent history, investors have demanded a more stable revenue stream and banks have therefore placed more emphasis on transaction fees, primarily loan fees but also including service charges on an array of deposit activities and ancillary services (international banking, foreign exchange, insurance, investments, wire transfers, etc.). Lending activities, however, still provide the bulk of a commercial bank's income.

In the past 10 years American banks have taken many measures to ensure that they remain profitable while responding to increasingly changing market conditions. First, this includes the Gramm-Leach-Bliley Act, which allows banks again to merge with investment and insurance houses.

Merging banking, investment, and insurance functions allows traditional banks to respond to increasing consumer demands for "one-stop shopping" by enabling cross-selling of products (which, the banks hope, will also increase profitability). Second, they have expanded the use of risk-based pricing from business lending to consumer lending, which means charging higher interest rates to those customers that are considered to be a higher credit risk and thus increased chance of default on loans. This helps to offset the losses from bad loans, lowers the price of loans to those who have better credit histories, and offers credit products to high risk customers who would otherwise been denied credit.

Third, they have sought to increase the methods of payment processing available to the general public and business clients. These products include debit cards, pre-paid cards, smart-cards, and credit cards. These products make it easier for consumers to conveniently make transactions and smooth their consumption over time (in some countries with under-developed financial systems, it is still common to deal strictly in cash, including carrying suitcases filled with cash to purchase a home). However, with convenience there is also increased risk that consumers will mismanage their financial resources and accumulate excessive debt. Banks make money from card products through interest payments and fees charged to consumers and transaction fees to companies that accept the cards.

The banking industry's main obstacles to increasing profits are existing regulatory burdens, new government regulation, and increasing competition from non-traditional financial institutions.

Bank Size Information

Top Ten Banking Groups in the World Ranked by Shareholder Equity ($m)

Rank	Country	Company	Shareholder equity ($m)
1	United States	Bank of America	138510 $mln
2	United States	Citigroup	127113 $mln
3	United Kingdom	HSBC	108352 $mln
4	Japan	Mitsubishi UFJ Financial Group	93913 $mln
5	France	Credit Agricole Group	65137 $mln
6	United Kingdom	Royal Bank of Scotland Group	64453 $mln
7	France	BNP Paribas	56610 $mln
8	Spain	Banco Santander	53640 $mln
9	Japan	Mizuho Financial Group	52243 $mln

The 2006 bank atlas was compiled from commercial banks' annual reports and financial statements for 2006 and 2005. Figures in U.S. dollars.

Top Ten Banking Groups in the World Ranked by Assets

Figures in U.S. dollars, and as at end-2004

Rank	Country	Company	Assets (US $)
1	United Kingdom	HSBC Holdings	1,861 billion
2	Switzerland	UBS	1,533 billion
3	United States	Citigroup	1,400 billion
4	Japan	Mizuho Financial Group	1,296 billion
5	France	Credit Agricole Group	1,243 billion
6	France	BNP Paribas	1,234 billion
7	United States	JPMorgan Chase & Co.	1,157 billion
8	Germany	Deutsche Bank	1,144 billion
9	United Kingdom	Royal Bank of Scotland	1,119 billion
10	United States	Bank of America	1,110 billion

Top Ten Banks in the World Ranked by Market Capitalization

Figures in Euros, and as at 22 November 2007

Rank	Country	Company	Market Capitalisation (Eur)
1	China	Industrial and Commercial Bank of China	230.880 billion
2	China	China Construction Bank	154.295 billion
3	China	Bank of China	141.466 billion
4	UK	HSBC Holdings	137.869 billion
5	US	Bank of America	128.430 billion
6	US	Citigroup	105.820 billion

Contd...

Rank	Country	Company	Market Capitalisation (Eur)*
7	US	JPMorgan Chase	94.609 billion
8	Spain	Banco Santander	92.438 billion
9	Italy	UniCredit	72.558 billion
10	US	Wells Fargo	69.036 billion

Top Ten Banking Groups in the World Ranked by Tier 1 Capital

Figures in U.S. dollars, and as at end-2005

Rank	Country	Company	Tier 1 Capital (US $)
1	UK	HSBC	79 billion
2	US	Citigroup	75 billion
3	US	Bank of America	73 billion
4	US	JP Morgan Chase	72 billion
5	Japan	Mitsubishi UFJ Financial Group	64 billion
6	France	Credit Agricole Group	60 billion
7	UK	Royal Bank of Scotland	48 billion
8	Japan	Sumitomo Mitsui Financial Group	40 billion
9	Japan	Mizuho Financial Group	39 billion
10	Spain	Banco Santander	38 billion

2

CREDIT RISK AND FINANCIAL PERFORMANCE ASSESSMENT

Pro forma financial performance evaluation of agricultural producers is an important issue for lenders, internal management and policy makers. Lenders strive to improve their credit risk management. Internal management is interested in understanding the financial impacts of alternative strategic decisions. And policy makers often assess the magnitude and distributional effects of alternative policies on the future financial performance of farm business.

Data limitations are a major impediment in assessing farm financial performance. Most traditional farm operations are private firms and thus, public traded equity information which can be converted into market valuation change is not available.

Moreover, historical loan performance data on agricultural loans such as past due and defaults are not readily available. These aspects present substantial methodological issues when establishing an independent variable to use in assessing future performance. Credit risk modeling and financial performance assessment have been remotivated and gained unprecedented academic attention in recent years (Barry 2001, Kachova and Barry 2005, Saunders and Allen 2002).

However, some of the new approaches and models have limitations when applied to agricultural producers. Adapting the models and approaches to utilize the available information of farm business needs careful attention and validation. In this paper, Altman's ' Z score model and ' Z score model are applied to farm accounting data for the detection of farm operating and financial difficulties. i.e., farms with high credit risk. The well-developed and widely used Altman models have not been applied to agricultural data.

The results are compared to an experienced based credit risk migration model (Splett, et al) and a logistic, lender-based model (Featherstone, Roessler, and Barry 2006). The experience based model is a primary model used in the current farm credit analysis. The logistic model is claimed for better statistical prediction accuracy and no binding assumption on multivariate normality (Altman 1968). Results from each of these models are compared across a common database of Midwestern grain farms.

Farms are grouped into different categories with different levels of financial. Instead of focusing on farm loan defaults, earned net worth growth rate (ENWGR) and term debt coverage ratio (TDCR) are used as two major indicators for financial stress situation of farm credit quality.

INTRODUCTION

Credit risk is the risk of default or of market value deterioration caused by the change of the obligator's credit quality. Default is a special case of credit quality downgrade when the credit quality deteriorates to the point where the obligator cannot meet its debt obligation. The borrower is either unable or unwilling to fulfill the terms promised under the loan contract. Farm credit risk is the uncertainty of paying the agricultural loan in full in a timely way.

Credit risk is a primary source of risk to financial institutions, and the holdings of capital including loan loss allowances and equity assets are main responses to such risk (Barry, 2001).

Credit risk evaluation in agricultural loans is important to farmers, agricultural lenders, and policy makers. More accurate credit risk evaluation leads to more precise loan pricing, lower loss rates, and reduced capital management costs. Agricultural lenders may benefit directly from making farm loan decisions efficiently and consistently through objective, numerically-based credit risk evaluation. With improved credit risk models, lenders can monitor loan portfolio loss exposure, make appropriate reserve policies, and meet safety and soundness regulation requirements. Also, the contingent costs from regulations, government loan programs, and taxpayers who ultimately bear the costs of risk bearing are less.

When agricultural lenders make loan decisions, they have asymmetric information about their borrowers and they cannot get external sources such as rating agencies data or publicly traded company stock data. Access and availability to high-quality, historical loan data for agricultural borrowers has been a primary issue in estimating and evaluating credit risk and financial performance models. In general, the two approaches have been to use lender data or farm accounting data (Miller and LaDue 1989).

The selection of the dependent variable, usually defaulted loans or problematic borrowers, for lender data models is usually constructed from real data. Statistically-based credit scoring models, such as linear probability model, discriminant analysis model, Logit model and Probit model can be applied to determine the factors that contribute to credit risk (Turvey, 1991).

However statistically-based models do not always give better prediction of credit risk and defaults than experience-based models (Splett, Barry, Dixon and Ellinger, 1994). Loan data are biased on the aspect that lenders only keep records on the accepted loans, but not the rejected applications which are often the problematic borrowers. Studies utilizing farm accounting data do not suffer from this bias and are generated from more random sampling since they do not discard problematic borrowers.

But, they can be exposed to survival bias due to the voluntary nature of the membership in state-record keeping associations. Moreover, the definition of the independent variable used in these models is also problematic. Often thresholds of specific financial ratios are used to measure performance.

An issue not addressed in previous studies is the ability of credit evaluation models to evaluate performance across alternative data. Statistical performance is often represented within the estimation sample or data, but there is little evidence regarding the generalization of the models to alternative data. Accounting data for a 5 year panel of farms are used to evaluate and compare measures of credit risk and financial performance across models developed with a different data set

To address this lack of lender-side data, credit risk migration analysis (Barry, Escalante and Ellinger, 2002) and option pricing approaches (Katchova and Barry, 2005) have been utilized to estimate farmers' credit risk. The migration approach is an extension of traditional financial ratio analysis and has several applications in farm credit risk analysis (Barry, Escalante and Ellinger, 2002). Since the classification cutoff values are based on experience, this approach still has the characteristics of experience based models.

The option pricing approaches also need to be applied with caution. First, the strength of option pricing approach is to transform equity market value into assets market value through Black-Scholes-Merton option pricing formula (Black and Scholes, 1973; Merton, 1974). Since farms are private firms, publicly traded and observable equity data are unavailable. Therefore, the mean and variance of farm assets values estimated using accounting data are not the required market value in the option pricing model for credit risk analysis.

Katchova and Barry applied the approach using farm accounting data, but only required a minimum of two annual data points to characterize the distribution and estimate the variance. This method is not likely robust nor comparable to using daily stock price information to characterize the asset distribution as other corporate finance studies have done. Second, in the applied option pricing models, such as Creditmetrics and KMV, the actual defaults are collected.

Therefore, the model outputs can be mapped into long time series and large cross sectional database with the actual defaults to generate the proper credit score. Without extensive historical data and cross sectional defaults, the option pricing model may not be statistically sound.

The overall objective of the paper is to evaluate and compare well-accepted models applied in corporate finance: the Z score models (Altman), with major models applied in agricultural finance: the experience-based credit scoring model (EBCSM) and the logistic model employed by Featherstone, Roessler, and Barry (FRB). If the farm stress can be modeled and predicted with farmer side accounting data, then the likelihood of being default is signaled to borrowers, lenders and relative policy makers. The Z score models and FRB's model were developed with the aid of lender data. EBSCM used an experience based model to assess performance. Specific objectives of this paper are:

1. to apply a well-defined and well-accepted credit risk model in corporate finance-Altman's Z score models to farm performance and credit risk analysis.
2. to compare the classifications, ranks and correlations of alternative credit scoring models using a common database, and
3. to investigate the relationship between credit score and future financial performance and stress.

In the following sections, the previous farm credit risk studies are reviewed and Altman's Z score models and the farm credit models are summarized. By developing Altman's Z score models and agricultural credit models with farm accounting data, the stress indicators are tested by assessing the statistical characteristics and changing trends among different risk groups. The models are compared and used to predict farm financial stress.

LITERATURE REVIEW

In generally terms, credit risk measurement approaches can be classified into three categories. The first categories are the "expertise" or "experience" models, for example the 5C's approach.

They are judgmental-based analysis with lender's experience and borrower's repayment history. This kind of approaches is time and labor intensive and often ratio somewhat arbitrary thresholds are established. The subjective assessment may not be statistically correlated to risk. However, the approach it is the most commonly used at commercial banks (Ellinger, Splett and Barry).

The second general category is statistically-based methods including the linear model, the Logit model, the

Probit model and the discriminant analysis model. These models estimate either a credit risk score or a probability of default for distinguishing borrowers (Sanders and Allen, 2002). Usually lender-side loan data are used. Among all statistically-based models, Altman's Z score models were one of the fist to be developed and are still being used by lenders and practitioners.

The criticism of statistical models includes the lacking of theoretical backup, linearity and distribution assumptions, and the ability of models to generalize to data not in the estimation sample.

In the third general category, more recent approaches have been developed by using mark-to-market data. The option pricing theory developed by Black, Scholes and Merton is the core of this type of models (Blank and Scholes, 1973; Merton, 1974). Since the market value fluctuation of borrower's assets is the fundamental source of credit risk and the fast moving changes in borrower's conditions cannot be captured by accounting data, the observable information from the stock market is a reliable evidence to predict borrower's credit worthiness.

The leading applications of the option pricing models are CreditMetrics© by J.P. Morgan and KMV© by Moody's. A good review of CreditMetrics and KMV models can be drawn from Crouhy, Galai and Mark (2000). Consistency of credit evaluation at agricultural banks was examined by Ellinger, Splett, and Barry (1992) with survey data from 717 agricultural banks. Their results showed large degree of dispersion in the use, implementation and design of lender credit scoring models.

It indicated the lack of efficient data and uniform model for lenders to evaluate the creditworthiness of agricultural borrowers. The models compared in this study were primarily experience based models.

Turvey (1991) compared four statistically based models: linear probability, discriminant method, Logit and Probit models using farm loan observations in Canada. The results show that the model predictive accuracies do not have significant differences among the four approaches. Ziari, Leatham and Turvey (1995) used actual loan data to evaluate the risk classification performance of parametric statistical models with nonparametric models. They concluded that two types of models only differ slightly in the classifying accuracy.

This study utilizes and compares the Altman's Z score models, EBSCM and FRB using a five-year farmer panel. The Altman model was first proposed by Altman in 1968 and then extended in 1977 and 2004 (Altman, 1968; 1977; 2004). One of the extended model, known as ZETA model is widely applied by finance business practitioners. The model is also extended to firms not traded publicly and to the non-manufacturing firms. The model specifications are described in the following section.

MODEL SPECIFICATION

This study compares four models. Since the original Altman's Z score model is applicable to publicly traded entities and requires stock market data, this study utilizes two extended models: Altman's ' Z score model developed for private firm and Altman's ' Z score model developed for non-manufacture type private firms (Altman, 2004). The experience based model EBSCM and the statistically based FRB model are the third and fourth models used to rank, classify and compare farms.

Altman's

Z Score model and Z Score Model Altman's Z score model uses five dependent variables out of the original 22 after sample selection and variable selection.

X_1 = working capital / total assets,

X_2 = retained earnings / total assets,

X_3 = earnings before interest and taxes / total assets,

X_4 = total equity / total liabilities,

X_5 = sales / total assets, and

Z = overall index

X_1 is a measure of the net liquid assets of farm relative to the total capitalization. Working capital is the difference between current assets and current liabilities. This financial ratio considers the liquidity and size characteristics explicitly. Usually a shrinking X_1 indicates consistent operating losses of farm. X_2 is a ratio that measures the cumulative profitability over time.

This ratio reports the cumulative share of farm's net earnings net of family living withdrawals and income taxes reinvested for next year. A relatively young farmer probably shows lower X_2 than older farmers. X_3 and X_4 measures the farmer's profitability and solvency. X_5 the capital turnover ratio is a measure of the management's efficiency. It illustrates the sales generating capability of assets employed on the farm. With equation (1), a 'Z score is computed for each farm in each year.

Altman's 'Z score equation's weights and classification boundaries are generated from the discriminant analysis. This study adopts the same weights and boundaries to investigate the direct application of the significant statistical characteristics on the farm stress indicators. In the Altman's 'Z score model the lower boundary is 1.23 and the upper boundary is 2.9. A below 1.23 'Z score indicates high credit risk and an above 2.9 'Z score indicates low credit risk. Therefore farms are grouped into three different credit risk classes.

Another extension Altman made on his original model is called 'Z score model (Altman, 2004). The difference between 'Z and 'Z is the elimination of the last variable X_5- an industry-sensitive ratio in equation (1). The weights changed as well. The purpose of 'Z score model is to minimize the potential industry effect which is more likely to take place when X_5 is included. For the farm sample, the moments and distributional properties of this ratio X_5 vary the most from Altman's sample. For example, the average for successful borrowers in Altman's study is 1.9 whereas the average for the farm sample is 0.27. But eliminating the asset turnover ratio provokes the understanding of credit risk change without the influence of farm and business types.

A below 1.1'Z score indicates high credit risk and an above 3.15 'Z score indicates low credit risk. Farms are grouped into three risk classes with the computed'Z scores.

EXPERIENCE BASED CREDIT RISK MODEL (EBCRM)

EBCRM is a credit scoring method developed by Splett et al. to classify farms. They used borower data provided by the Farm Credit Bank of St. Louis. Instead of using real loan repayment performance classification, loans are classified by the borrower's farm business performance. With an experience-based model, FFSC dependent variables, variables weights, and interval cutoff points were established and a credit score was computed for each loan.

An important contribution of their study is the credit scoring method to classify the loans by farm performance measures, i.e., the FFSC financial measures. It initialized the credit risk evaluation from the borrower's side. Five key measure variables are chosen by the farm lending expert panel.

They are liquidity, profitability, repayment capacity, and efficiency. For each variable, five interval ranges are defined (See Table 1). Each farm has five scores on liquidity, solvency, profitability, repayment capacity and financial efficiency accordingly. These five scores are weighted to generate a total score between 1 and 5. Then, each farm is grouped to a credit risk class.

Equation (3) provides the weights for the factors. Unlike ' Z score and ' Z score, the weights are generated from experience. The 5 risk classes used in the original study are mapped into 3 categories for purposes of comparing the Altman models. Classes 1 and 2 are mapped into the lowest risk class, classes 3 and 4 into moderate risk and class 5 is the high risk class.

Binary Logistic Model for Estimating the Probability of Default (FRB)

The most recent statistically based credit risk model is the logistic model estimating the probability of default of 157,853 loans within the Seventh Farm Credit District (Featherstone, Roessler and Barry). They utilized historical financial origination ratios based on underwriting standards to predict the probability of default of different loan types. The estimated probability of default is mapped into a similar default risk grid of S&P publicly rated firms for appropriate loan pricing. The results indicate that repayment capacity, owner equity and working capital are important determinants of probability of default.

The FRB model defines default as a payment being ninety days or more past due at least once since origination. This is the traditional and widely-applied definition for default. Two classes of default and not-default construct the binary dependent variable. Three origination ratios are used as the independent variables: Capital Debt Repayment

Capacity Percentage (CDRC), Owner Equity Percentage (OE), and Working Capital Percentage (WC). The regression results for the overall model-show that all three ratios are significant in the model.

With equation 4, the probability of default is estimated for each farm. FRB chose a cutoff value of 2% for classifying default. The proposed FCS guidelines reported in their study suggest a cutoff of between 0.26 and 0.52 for BBB-loans. The grouping of three classes for FRB are based on PD cutoffs of 0.50% and 2%.

Stress Indicators

This study adopts the results from Zech and Pederson (2003) as the stress indicators. The first stress indicator is the Term Debt Coverage Ratio (TDCR). The second stress indicator is the Earned Net Worth Growth Rate (ENWGR). The Term Debt coverage ratio calculation is the standard established by FFSC. Earned net worth growth is calculated as:

Similar to Zech and Pederson, the stress indicators are calculated as averages. The averaging of the dependent variables removes some of the year-to-year volatility inherent in farm income and provides a slightly longer-term stress index.

DATA

This study uses the annual farm data from 2000 through 2004 provided by the Illinois Farm Business and Farm Management (FBFM) Association. FBFM is an informative database with Illinois farmers' financial information. Cost and market values of assets and liabilities are available as well as farm and nonfarm income and expenditure data. There are 399 sole proprietors that meet the consistency and field staff validation criteria to be included in a comparative data set over the entire five year sample. Verification procedures included certifications on cost and market asset valuation; income certification; and farm and nonfarm cash flow expenditure validation. Previous studies using the FBFM data typically only utilize a 2 year continuous sample (Kachova and Barry 2005, Phillips and Kachova 2005). A more consistent analysis result is expected since this study does not include the farms that drop out or enter in the database during a 5-year period. Moreover, the extended sample allows for the testing of model performance in years subsequent to initial credit evaluation and scoring.

The average ENWGR ranged from a low of-1% in 2001 to a high of 5% in 2004, while the average TDRC ranged from 2.74 in 2003 to 21.38 in 2001. The average Z score and the proportion of high risk borrowers for the Altman 1 model are substantially larger than the Z score for the Altman 2 model. This is primarily due to the inclusion of the capital turnover (sales to asset) ratio. Agricultural businesses tend to be more capital intensive and have higher proportions of assets relative to sales.

For example, the average ratio for agricultural borrows in the sample is 0.27 whereas in the Altman original study the average was 1.9. Since the coefficient on this ratio is approximately 1.0, the result is a difference of over 1.5 in the calculated Z score and hence, a higher proportion of borrowers classified as high risk. Similar to FRB results, a substantial proportion of borrowers are grouped in the 2 to 2.5% range and thus, a higher proportion of borrowers are classified in the high risk FRB class.

RESULTS

Comparisons of the classification results over the entire 5-year period are provided in Table 3. Values on the diagonals of each sub matrix indicate the risk categories are similar between the two models. Large inconsistencies occur with the Altman models. For example, 135 of the 813 borrowers classified as high risk for Altman 1 are classified as low risk in the Altman 2 model. Another major discrepancy occurs between the FRB model and Altman 2 model. Almost 10% of the borrowers classified as low risk in the Altman 2 model are classified as high risk in the FRB model. The classification procedures are not standardized across the models.

Another method to compare the models is to measure simple correlation coefficients of the raw scores of each model. The Spearman rank correlation coefficients for the models are provided in Table 4. The rank correlation among all the models is very strong ranging from-0.79 between EBSCM and Altman 2 to 0.966 between the two Altman models. Indications are that the ranking of farms is similar across the models whereas the distribution and classifications of the models differ.

Effective risk rating models should have a strong relationship to future financial performance and be able to identify future financial stress. Two stress measures are calculated in each year-earned net worth growth (ENWGR) and term debt and capital replacement ratio (TDCR). To remove some of the year-to-year variability prevalent in farming, the measures are averaged over a two-year period.

The results for credit score classifications generated in 2000 for periods 2001-02, 2002-03, and 2003-04 are provided in Table 5. The mean values and significant differences of means across credit rating classes for each of the stress indicators are provided. In general, the directional effects are as expected. The low risk models result in stronger earnings and repayment performance in future periods. As expected the significance tends to decline as the prediction time frame lengthens.

Poor loan performance is often dictated by extremely stressed conditions. Another approach to assess and compare the models is to establish a stress threshold where the performance ratio is categorized as high risk (Zech and Pederson). For each of the two ratios, a cutoff threshold is used to separate high risk farms from other farms. The values for ENWGR and TDCR are 0.00 and 1.00 respectively. Credit scores are then used to evaluate the proportion of farms that exceed the threshold in future periods. The mean results and statistical differences based on credit scores in 2000 are reported. Each percentage value represents the proportion of the 399 farms that did not exceed the stress threshold in each respective period. For example, the 32.47% value for ENWGR for 2001-02 indicates that for all farms classified as low risk with the Altman 1 model in 2000, 32.47% of the farms will be below the stress threshold of 0 in 2001-02. Again, the general direction of each of the models is consistent with expectations. The EBCSM was the only model that exhibited statistical differences in each year for ENWGR.

A final comparison among the models involves estimating a simple logit model measuring the relationship between the raw credit score (or PD) and the high risk threshold classifications for each future period. Graphical results are provided in Figures 1 and 2. The steeper the curve, the stronger the relationship between the credit score and future financial performance and stress.

The agricultural models (EBCSM and FRB) tend to have stronger relationships with both the earnings and repayment stress indicators. The Altman models did not have a strong relationship with future repayment analysis. This is likely due to the inclusion of repayment capacity in the agricultural models and the linkage over time of repayment capacity.

CONCLUSION

This study applies the Altman's ' Z (Altman 1) score and ' Z (Altman 2) corporate finance scoring models to agricultural producers and compares the results to an experience based and statistically-based agricultural models. With the Illinois farm accounting data, farms are grouped into high, medium, and low credit risk levels under each model. The classification effects are tested and the results show that all models can classify farms into different risk levels. Two stress indicators are used to assess the relationships the models have with future performance.

In general the models were highly correlated and resulted in consistent ranks. However, the distribution of the scores and classification rules of the models differed. The models tended to be related to short-term future performance, but the relationship declined over time.

The Altman models do not perform as well and some inconsistencies occur in classification. This is likely due to the inherent differences of financial ratios between corporate borrowers and agricultural firms. An extension of this analysis would be to re- weight the discriminant function for agricultural purposes.

GETTING READY FOR BASEL II

Gary Rice breaks down the latest US proposals on Basel II and explains why lawyers must be aware of them to advise clients adequately On March 22 2006, the Board of Governors of the Federal Reserve System released the text of a proposed rule for implementing Basel II: the revised risk-based capital guidelines developed by the Basel Committee on Banking Regulations and Supervisory

Practices. Only the largest (with total assets of $250 billion or more) and most internationally active (with $10 billion or more in foreign assets) US banking organizations will be required to comply with the proposed rule when it is finalized. There are 11 such US banking organisations, and it is expected that approximately 20 additional US banking organizations will voluntarily seek to qualify.

The proposed rule is 448 pages long and full of acronyms and mathematical formulas. A lawyer flipping through it might wonder what role lawyers could conceivably have in interpreting such a document. Certainly, much of the work of implementing the proposed rule at US banking organizations will fall to risk managers rather than to lawyers. Daunting as the proposed rule may be, however, lawyers that represent large US financial institutions will need to familiarize themselves with it because it will influence the way many types of transactions are structured, particularly derivatives and securitizations, and because banks will look to lawyers to assist them with complying with the extensive new public disclosures that the new rules will require.

The existing risk-based capital rules use a simple approach to assessing credit risk: assets are grouped into a few categories based on the type of obligor (or, in a few cases, the type of obligation) and assigned risk-weights ranging from 0% to 100%. Off-balance sheet liabilities that have credit risk are first multiplied by a credit conversion factor, ranging from 0% to 100%, and then risk weighted based on the type of obligor. The simplicity of the rules is best illustrated by the fact that virtually all claims on private sector companies are assigned the same 100% risk weight.

The proposed rule attempts to be much more risk sensitive. For the purposes of setting risk-based capital requirements, the proposed rule divides credit and equity exposures into four categories: wholesale, retail, securitizations and equity.

Wholesale

Wholesale exposures cover most exposures to companies and government entities that are managed on an individual basis and are not either securitizations or equity exposures. Banks would be required to estimate certain risk parameters, which are then inputted into a formula that is based on a value-at-risk methodology and is prescribed by the regulation. The proposed rule would require banks to have a "comprehensive risk parameter quantification system that produces accurate, timely, and reliable estimates of the risk parameters".

It would also require the models used to estimate risk parameters to be "transparent, well supported and documented". The first risk parameter is probability of default (PD), which is the likelihood (expressed as a percentage) that a wholesale obligor will default within one year. Each bank would develop a rating system that estimates the PD of each obligor based on data such as historic and projected financial performance, industry risk and non-financial contingencies such as labour problems. The risk rating system must have at least seven PD grades and each wholesale obligor will be assigned a PD based on the rating grade.

The PD would apply to all of the obligor's obligations, without regard to the type of loan or the existence of collateral. In many areas of the proposed rule, the regulators have restricted outcomes to ensure that capital requirements do not fall too far. In this case, for non-government entities, the floor PD is 0.03. The second risk parameter is the expected loss (expressed as a percentage of the expected exposure at the time of default) given a default (ELGD). Banks would either estimate the ELGD of each exposure or assign-ELGDs to groups of exposures that have similar characteristics. The ELGD would reflect not only the net present value of the cash flows that would be lost in the event of a default, but mitigation of that loss due to the existence of collateral and costs associated with the loan workout process.

The third risk parameter, loss given default (LGD) is the same as ELGD except that it is the expected loss, given a default, if the default occurs during an economic downturn. The proposed rule does not require banks to reflect geographical, industry, sector or other concentrations in calculating LDG.

Banks are given the choice of estimating the LGD of individual or groups of exposures, or using a simple formula for converting ELGD to LGD. The regulators include a different correlative factor in the risk-based capital formula for high volatility commercial real estate exposures, requiring more capital for them on the theory that risk for such loans is more highly correlated with economic downturns.

The fourth risk parameter, known as EAD, is the estimated dollar exposure at the time of default and, except for derivatives and certain other types of assets, will generally be the carrying value of the asset. The final risk parameter is the number of years of remaining maturity.

Once a bank estimates all of the risk parameters for an exposure, it inputs them into the risk-based capital formula for wholesale exposures that is prescribed in table two of the proposed rule and multiplies the result by the EAD. This is done for each wholesale exposure and the sum of the results is the dollar risk-based capital requirement for those exposures.

Retail

Retail exposures are exposures to individuals and small businesses that a bank manages in segments rather than on an individual basis, as is the case with wholesale exposures.

Under the proposed rule, the bank would first divide its retail exposures into three groups: residential mortgage exposures, qualifying revolving exposures (such as credit card loans) and other. These three groups are assigned different correlative factors in the risk-based capital formula for retail exposures because their risk correlates differently with economic downturn conditions.

The bank would then divide the retail exposures into segments with similar risk characteristics (such as loan-to-value ratios, credit scores, collateral type, geography, loan terms and structure). For each segment, the bank would estimate the PD, ELGD, LGD and EAD, just as it would do for wholesale exposures. The PD, ELGD or LGD of a segment would be adjusted to reflect collateral, if any. The bank would then input the risk parameters for each exposure into the risk-based capital formula for retail exposures that is prescribed in table two of the proposed rule and multiply the result by the EAD.

The proposed rule acknowledges that the risk-based capital formulas for wholesale and retail exposures are less sophisticated than many banks currently use because they do not take into account the extent to which risks within the bank's portfolio are correlated with one another. This simplification was necessary in order to have formulas that could be applied across a range of banks with very different portfolios.

The proposed rule assumes that each bank's portfolio is diversified. To the extent that a bank's portfolio has asset or geographic concentrations, an adjustment would be made to its capital requirement as part of the supervisory process.

The advanced notice of proposed rulemaking, which was issued in 2003, would have required banks to hold capital against both expected losses and unexpected losses. Many comments argued that expected losses are more appropriately covered by the allowance for loan loss reserves. The regulators accepted this point and in the proposed rule the capital requirements are based on unexpected losses. However, the proposed rule would also require each bank to compare its expected credit losses (the product of PD, ELGD and EAD for the exposure or segment) against its loan loss allowances and deduct any excess loss estimate 50% from tier one and 50% from tier two. Similarly, if loan loss allowances exceed expected credit losses, the bank would add the excess to tier two capital up to 0.6% of credit risk-weighted assets. The regulators regard this as equivalent to the limited extent to which credit reserves are included in tier two capital under the current risk-based capital guidelines.

The proposed rule also includes a scaling factor that is intended to ensure that the rule does not permit required capital to fall by more than 10%. The most recent quantitative impact study, which 26 banks participated in, showed that the new capital guidelines would result in a dollar-weighted average reduction of 15.5% in risk- based capital requirements at participating banks. Half of the participating banks reported reductions in tier one risk-based capital requirements of over 31%. It is unclear whether a similar reduction will occur under the final rules, which will not be fully implemented at any bank until 2012.

The scaling factor in the proposed rule is 1.06. Total credit risk-weighted assets resulting from the application of the formulas will be multiplied by this factor for purposes of determining a bank's total credit risk-weighted asset amount. Operational risk-weighted assets (discussed below) would be added to this amount and the bank's qualifying capital would be divided by this total to arrive at a risk-based capital ratio. If in the course of implementation it appears that this scaling factor is insufficient to prevent the new guidelines from causing an unacceptable drop in capital requirements, then the regulators will increase the scaling factor or otherwise adjust the formulas.

Another way in which the proposed rule guards against a sudden drop in capital is to require a bank to maintain the capital required under both the current rules and the new rules for the first year in which it implements the new rules. For the next three years, the bank will be required to hold at least 95%, 90% and 80%, respectively, of the capital required under the current rules.

Securitization

The proposed rule defines securitizations as tranched exposures to a pool of underlying financial exposures. If the underlying exposure is not a financial exposure, as might be the case, for example, with a project finance deal, then it would be treated as wholesale exposure. Synthetic securitizations would generally be treated in the same manner as traditional securitizations. The proposed rule does not permit banks to estimate the risk parameters for securitizations. Instead risk weights for securitization exposures are based on ratings or on the risk-based capital requirement for the underlying exposures.

If the securitization exposure is rated, or is senior to a rated tranche, then the ratings-based approach must be used. The proposed rule includes tables that provide risk weights based on whether the securitization exposure is long or short term, its rating, its granularity (whether there are six or more underlying exposures) and its seniority (whether the exposure is senior to all other tranches). For example, a long-term exposure with the lowest investment grade rating with a negative designation (BBB-for example) is assigned a risk weight of 100%.

A long-term exposure one category below investment grade is assigned a risk weight of 425%.

If the exposure is not rated, and if it is an eligible asset-backed commercial paper programme exposure, then the bank may use the internal assessment approach, in which case the bank maps its internal credit assessment of a securitization exposure to an equivalent external credit rating from a rating agency. This rating is then used to derive a risk weight from the tables for the ratings-based approach.

If neither of the above approaches is available, the bank may use the supervisory formula approach. However, that is available only if the bank is able to calculate seven inputs, one of which is the risk-based capital requirement and estimated credit loss for each of the underlying exposures. If this approach is not available because the inputs cannot be calculated, the bank must deduct the exposure from capital.

The risk-based capital requirement for a securitization cannot exceed the sum of the risk-based capital requirement for the underlying exposures and the expected credit loss for those exposures (the latter on the theory that if the exposures were on the balance sheet the bank would have to keep reserves or capital against them).

Equity

Under the proposed rule, banks would determine the risk-based capital requirement for equity exposures under one of two approaches. The internal models approach would allow banks to use their own models, once approved by the regulators, for estimating the risk of loss on equity exposures.

The proposed rule would not require that any particular type of model be used. However, the risk weights resulting from an internal models approach would be subject to a floor of 200% for publicly-traded equity exposures and a floor of 300% for privately-traded equity exposures.

The second approach, called the simple risk-weight approach, would assign the adjusted carrying value of an equity exposure a risk weight of 300% for publicly-traded equity exposures, and 400% for privately-traded equity exposures.

The adjusted carrying value, in the case of on-balance sheet equity exposures, would be calculated by removing unrealized gains that are excluded from capital (65% of the gain). For off-balance sheet items, the adjusted carrying value would be the amount of on-balance sheet exposure that would change in fair value to the same extent as the off-balance sheet item for a given small change in the price of the underlying equity exposure, less the adjusted carrying value of the on-balance sheet component of the exposure.

Equity derivatives would generally meet the definition of both an equity exposure (because of the underlying asset) and a wholesale exposure (because of credit exposure to the counterparty). If a bank uses the internal models approach, the risk-based capital requirement generally would be the sum of the requirement for the two parts of the exposure. The proposed rule also provides for the adjustment of the capital requirement to account for hedged exposures.

The proposed rule offers three approaches to determining the capital requirements for equity exposure to investment funds. The full look-through approach calls for the risk-based capital requirement to be calculated by determining the requirement for each underlying exposure. The simple modified look-through approach calculates capital based on the highest risk weight that applies to any exposure in the fund.

Finally, where fund documents indicate maximum percentages that may be invested in different types of exposures, a bank may use the alternative modified lookthrough approach, which assumes that the fund will invest the maximum amount permitted in the highest risk weight exposure, and works backward until 100% of the fund is accounted for.

Operational Risk

In addition to the capital requirements for credit and equity exposures, the proposed rule would assign a specific risk-based capital requirement for operational risk, which is the risk of loss, exclusive of insurance and tax effects, from events "associated with internal fraud; external fraud; employment practices and workplace safety; clients, products, and business practices; damage to physical assets; business disruption and system failures; or execution, delivery and process management".

The proposed rule would require banks to "establish and document a process to identify, measure, monitor, and control operational risk in bank products, activities, processes, and systems".

Banks must choose a value-at-risk methodology and produce an estimate of operational risk at the one-year 99.9th percentile confidence level. Also, the methodology must cover expected and unexpected operational loss, unless the bank can show that the former is covered by offsets, such as operational risk reserves.

Market Discipline

The regulators included market discipline as the third pillar of the proposed rule on the theory that, if banks are required to publicly disclose substantial information regarding their risk management processes, then the potential effect of such disclosures on the market for their securities would encourage them to have strong risk management processes. In adopting the proposed rule, the regulators brushed aside complaints that such disclosure would be too burdensome, not comparable across banks, and likely to be misinterpreted by the public.

The required disclosures are contained in a series of 11 tables at the end of the proposed rule. The disclosures are both extensive and detailed. For example, with respect to a bank's assessment of credit risk for wholesale exposures, the bank is required to not only describe the definitions, method and data for estimation and validation of each of the risk parameters, it is required to provide, across a number of PD grades, total EAD, exposure weighted ELGD and LDG, and exposure-weighted capital requirements.

It is also required to provide a comparison of risk parameter estimates against actual outcomes for both the preceding period and a longer period. This comparison would at a minimum be shown for the wholesale category and each retail category and, where appropriate, the bank should further decompose this to provide analysis of each risk parameter outcomes against estimates.

MEASURING AGGREGATE PROCESSPERFORMANCE USING AHP

Financial Institutions Center

The Wharton Financial Institutions Center provides a multi-disciplinary research approach to the problems and opportunities facing the financial services industry in its search for competitive excellence. The Center's research focuses on the issues related to managing risk at the firm level as well as ways to improve productivity and performance.

The Center fosters the development of a community of faculty, visiting scholars and Ph.D. candidates whose research interests complement and support the mission of the Center. The Center works closely with industry executives and practitioners to ensure that its research is informed by the operating realities and competitive demands facing industry participants as they pursue competitive excellence.

Copies of the working papers summarized here are available from the Center. If you would like to learn more about the Center or become a member of our research community, please let us know of your interest.

When one undertakes a benchmarking study, it is quite typical to collect performance data on a set of business processes from a variety of organizations. While one can compare efficiency on a process-by-process level, how can one compare the overall efficiency of one organization versus another using this process-level data? This note presents a methodology that combines tournament ranking and AHP approaches to create a ranking scheme that deals explicitly with missing data and ties in the tournament scheme. Keywords: AHP, Benchmarking, Process Efficiency

Social science and applied business research often uses indices to indicate the value of some phenomena. The question that repeatedly arises is how to bring together the various components to form a single index. In the case where the various components are measured along the same dimension and range, the most obvious method is to take an average score of the components. Such index creation often arises in the context of benchmarking studies.

Benchmarking studies typically involve the collection of a vast quantity of statistical, anecdotal, and qualitative information concerning the relative performance of various business processes within and between organizations. Thus, such benchmarking is at the heart of the modern reengineering a phenomenon that is sweeping through organizations throughout the world (Hammer and Champy, 1993; Davenport and Short, 1990).

More than just an interesting tool for industry, the ability to compare the relative merits of various business process designs is crucial in understanding the drivers of competitiveness and performance in organizations. The design of a business process is neither an input or output as it is neither created nor consumed as other inputs and outputs; rather, the design provide the structure for the creation and consumption of the existing inputs and outputs. The process, according to Morroni (1992), actually defines how capital and labor interact in order to produce outputs.

For example, Morroni provides an illustrative example in which there are ten ditch diggers with ten shovels. If an eleventh shovel is added, the process of ditch digging must be changed. That is, an additional shovel will not benefit the one-person, one-shovel process. The point here is that a process typically defines the relationship between capital and labor and thus, they are not immediately interchangeable. Thus, the process design defines the production technology for the organization.

Given that process designs are not the same as inputs like labor, how can processes be analyzed for their relative efficiency? For analyzing the relative efficiency of a single process, Frei and Harker (1995) present an extension of Data Envelopment Analysis (DEA) to incorporate process design characteristics. However, organizations are composed of multiple business processes. How is one organization compared to another when measuring business process-level data? This question is the focus of the current note.

This note presents a method for determining an index in the instance when each of the components is a relative ranking. That is, when there are a group of relative performance measures across a variety of measures, and it is necessary to aggregate these measures, what method of aggregation should be used? Taking an average is the most obvious thing to do, but there are several problems with this approach.

First, if the relative performance measures are ratio-scale numbers, then their average is meaningless theoretically (Saaty 1986). We present a method that allows for ratio-scale numbers and missing data to come up with an aggregation score or index. We then apply this method to a small to show how it is more suitable than considering average performance.

Using an Analytic Hierarchy Process (AHP)-like method, we present an alternative that is theoretically and practically superior to the most common index-creation scheme, especially when using relative measures. This method overcomes the problem of aggregating ratio-scale metrics and thus, is useful in wide array of social science and operations management contexts. The remainder of this note is structured as follows.

The next section will review the Frei and Harker (1996) method for analyzing the efficiency of a single process and will be followed by the description of the proposed method of aggregating these single process metrics to create organizational efficiency scores. The note will then conclude with the description of a small example of this method to demonstrate its superiority to existing methods.

ANALYZING SINGLE PROCESS EFFICIENCY

Frei and Harker (1996) describe an extension of Data Envelopment Analysis (DEA) to analyze the relative efficiency of a given business process across multiple organizations. Creating a process map is the standard first step in the evaluation of processes (Shostack, 1987; Kingman-Brundage, 1992).

However, even after a careful study of process maps has occurred, it is still difficult to determine how efficient a single process is or, from a group of processes, which is better. There is no existing methodology that helps us to formally compare processes. The technique developed by Frei and Harker builds on existing frontier estimation methods to provide a way to evaluate processes with multiple inputs and outputs, at least some of which have non- market values. The first step is to determine the relative efficiency of a given process, the other firms that might be used for benchmarking this process, and the managerial implications of the choices involved.

The work of Brockett and Golany (1996) introduces the concept, in the context of Data Envelopment Analysis (DEA), of organizing decision making units (DMUs) into subgroups in order to determine if one subgroup outperforms another. This logic is easily transferred to processes, where it is recognized that while all processes require the same categories of inputs to produce similar categories of outputs, there are vastly different ways of organizing the way in which the work occurs.

Brockett and Golany determine the efficient frontier for each subgroup in order to determine which input and output scenarios are dominant within each subgroup. Although it is easy to visually understand which process-design group is dominant in two dimensions, Brockett and Golany provide no means of determining this in higher dimensions. Thus, although Brockett and Golany's idea of comparing frontiers is useful in two dimensions, it is quite difficult in higher dimensions. Frei and Harker (1996) present a-methodology for comparing process groups in higher dimensions.

ANALYZING ORGANIZATIONAL PROCESS EFFICIENCY

The previous section outlined an approach for analyzing the efficiency of business processes on a process-by-process basis. However, organizations are a collection of such processes. How can these be aggregated to form an index of efficiency for the organization as a whole? This question is addressed herein.

A standard approach for aggregating data at an institutional or 'team' level is to conduct institutional comparisons is a tournament-ranking scheme. The first step in using a tournament ranking scheme is to develop a matrix of 'wins'; i.e. a matrix $W = (w_{ij})$ where each entry, w_{ij}, represents the number of times that Participant i beat Participant j. That is, if there are 10 participants there will be a 10x10 matrix such that each entry in the matrix $W = (w_{ij})$ represents the number of times Participant i performed better than Participant j. In the case where two participants have never competed against each other, the entries are left blank and treated as "missing data." This "missing data" can be handled by using the correction developed by Harker (1987).

In the case where Participant i outperforms Participant j for all of their common processes, a zero would be entered in cell w_{ij}, and the number of common processes entered in cell w_{ji}.

Traditionally, the second step in tournament ranking analysis is to develop a matrix of wins-to- losses where each entry is replaced with $_{jiijww}$. However, when considering the case where one participant wins all of the matches against another participant (i.e., $w_{ji} = 0$), the result is an undefined value as one entry in the wins-to-losses matrix.

Thus, this entry would state that Participant i is infinitely better than Participant j. In most cases, such infinite values make no practical sense.

In order to limit the value of the matrix elements, one can invoke the bounded scale property axiom in Saaty's (1986) Analytic Hierarchy Process. Thus, creating a bounded scale leads us to use Saaty's bounded reciprocal matrix approach to forming the matrix that represents the relative power of one organization or participant over the other (see Harker and Vargas 1987 for details).

Thus, rather than having each matrix entry as the number of wins divided by the number of losses or jiijww (where there would be potentially undefined entries), each entry is represented by, where represents the bound of how much better one organization is than another. The bound used in this note is the number proposed by Saaty (1986) (i.e., = 9).

This allows for an entry of 1 when two organizations have the same numbers of wins and losses and ranges from 1/ to for the range of possible performance scores when there are uneven wins and losses. Thus, if one participant wins all of the matches, that participant will have an entry of 9 in the wins-to-losses matrix, and the losing participant will have an entry of 1/9. Formally, the algorithm for the tournament-ranking scheme for aggregating process-level efficiency analyses is as follows:

Step 1

Determine the rank of each institution for each process using the process described in Frei and Harker (1995).

Step 2

Determine a matrix of "wins" and losses for each process where w_{ij} equals the number of processes for which institution i outranks institution j. Enter one for each diagonal entry.

Step 3

For each instance in which there are no competitions in common between two participants (i.e., $w_{ij} + w_{ji} = 0$), add 1 to the diagonal of the win-loss matrix for each participant and replace the two cells which correspond to the lack of competition with zeros.

Step 4

Scale the win-loss matrix with to ensure that one organization is not considered infinitely better than another is. Do not perform the scaling for "missing data" cells but rather keep their value as zero.

Step 5

Determine the eigenvector of the scaled win-loss matrix. This eigenvector contains the relative performance over each institution for the set of processes. In order to illustrate the algorithm, consider the following small example. Three competitors have competed against each other in up to four competitions.

The matrix shown in Table below represents the rank of each team in each competition. For example, in the second competition, Team C won and Team B came in second; Team A did not compete in the second competition. The mean rank is included in the last row to indicate the traditional measure for evaluating the best performer. According to the mean rank, the order of performance for the teams is A, C, and B. We will show how the rank from our methodology differs from this and more closely resembles relative performance.

Table:. Sample Matrix of Ranks

	Team A	Team B	Team C
Competition 1	1	2	
Competition 2	2	1	
Competition 3	1	2	
Competition 4	1	2	
Mean Rank	1	1.75	1.5

Table below represents the matrix of wins and losses for each team (Step 2). That is, each row represents the number of times that a team beat the competitor in the corresponding column. For example, Team A beat Team B twice. In addition, each column represents the number of times that a competitor lost to the competitor in the corresponding row. For example, Team C lost to Team B once. Notice that a one is entered for each diagonal entry.

Table:. Sample Matrix of Wins and Losses

	Team A	Team B	Team C
Team A	1	2	0
Team B	0	1	1
Team C	0	1	1

The next step is to determine which participants did not compete against each other (Step 3). In this example, Team A did not compete against Team C, and thus one must be added to the diagonal for Team A and Team C. In addition, a zero is recorded for each of the missing data locations. Next each entry is scaled according to the formula in order to determine the scaled matrix of wins-to-losses (Step 4). The scaled results are recorded in Table below.

Table: Scaled Matrix of Wins and Losses

	Team A	Team B	Team C
Team A	2	9	0
Team B	1/9	1	1
Team C	0	1	2

Finally, the eigenvector of the matrix is determined using the scaled data as shown in Table below. As can be seen in this table, the order of performance for the teams has changed in this method as compared to using the mean rank. This is because the mean performance does not adequately account for the situation when some competitions include only a subset of the teams.

In this example, Team C has a better mean score than Team B even though they split their head- to-head competitions. While Team B lost to Team A twice, this loss should not inform Team B's ranking relative to Team C as Team C did not compete against Team A. It could very well be that Team A is simply better than Team B and that Team B and Team C are equal to one another. The method described in this note produces this very result which we feel more accurately reflects the relative performance of this data.

Table: Eigenvector and Rankings

Eigenvector	Eigenvector Order	Mean Rank	Mean Rank Order	
Team A	0.82	1	1	1
Team B	0.09	2	1.75	3
Team C	0.09	2	1.5	2

The methodology just described generates a composite performance score for each team when competing across a number of competitions. As can be seen from the above example, simply using the average performance can be misleading, especially when there is missing data. The proposed method takes into account the missing data and more accurately produces a ranking which reflects relative performance.

AN EMPIRICAL EXAMPLE WITH THE BANKING INDUSTRY

In order to demonstrate the usefulness of the technique developed herein, we apply it to a data set from the banking industry. This data is a result of the retail banking study undertaken at the Wharton Financial Institutions Center. The retail banking study was aimed at understanding the drivers of firm performance and the relationship between industry trends and the experiences of the retail banking labor force.

Participation in the study required substantial time and effort on the part of organizations. Therefore, commitment to participation was sought by approaching the 70 largest U.S. BHCs directly, and, in the second half of 1994, the participation of one retail banking entity from each BHC was requested. Fifty-seven BHCs agreed to participate. Of these, seven BHCs engaged the participation of two or more retail banks in the BHC, giving 64 retail banks in total.

Multiple questionnaires were delivered to each organization in this sample. Questionnaires ranged from 10 to 30 pages, and were designed to target the "most informed respondent" (Huber and Power, 1985) in the bank in a number of areas, including business strategy, technology, human resource management and operations, and the design of business processes. Altogether, the entire survey of retail banking covers 121 BHCs, and 135 banks, which together comprise over 75% of the total industry, as measured by asset size. The scope and scale of this survey make it the most comprehensive survey to date on the retail banking industry.

For this paper, we analyze the set of retail banks for which we have data on process performance and financial measures. This reduces our sample to forty-five retail banks. The process performance measures used in this paper rely on the ability to grade a firm for each individual process relative to the other banks in the study. That is, for each firm there are grades for up to eleven processes. The methodology used to grade the processes is described in Frei and Harker (1996), which demonstrates an extension of DEA to analyze the relative efficiency of a given business process across multiple organizations.

After determining the process-level efficiency score for each institution, the grade is determined by normalizing the efficiency scores to a scale of 0% to 100%, with the efficient banks scoring 100%. Before we present our analysis, we need a formal description of a production process. A production process is the way in which work is organized and inputs are consumed in order to produce outputs. For example, a process might be the way in which a checking account is opened. The inputs consumed are the labor (platform representative) and capital (information technology), and the outputs produced are the opening of the account in a way that is convenient for the customer (in terms of customer time involved and when they have access to their money).

In order to understand the process of opening a checking account, we need to know the steps involved, the order of these steps, the way in which people are involved, and the role of technology. For our analysis, we look at a process as a mapping from inputs to outputs and identify the critical design issues that lead to greater value.

For each of the eleven processes in this study, the efficiency analysis described in Frei and Harker (1996) has been performed. This analysis determines the efficiency with which each bank produces a set of outputs from a set of inputs. The categories of inputs and outputs for each process are shown in Table.

For each process, the banks have been ranked according to their efficiency score and thus there are up to eleven rankings for each of the banks. The results of this individual process analysis are then aggregated using the methodology described herein to create an institutional aggregate process efficiency score. The aggregated score is used to analyze the role of process efficiency in describing performance of a bank.

Does Process Efficiency Matter?

While there is a significant body of theoretical (Morroni, 1992) and anecdotal and Short, 1990) evidence on the importance of process management, there is little statistical evidence that process management matters with respect to the 'bottom line' of the institution. We show that, while no individual process is correlated with firm performance, the aggregate measure of process performance is correlated with firm performance.

We consider the relationship between the process efficiency of a bank, as measured by its aggregate process performance, and the financial performance of the institution. Deciding on a single measure of financial performance of a firm is difficult. We have consulted with industry and academic experts and have come up with five financial performance measures that fall into roughly three categories.

The first category is the most traditional, return on investment. In this category, we have return on assets

(ROA) and return on equity (ROE). The second category contains the market measures of market-to-book ratio and Tobin's Q. The final category contains a profit efficiency measure derived by Berger and Mester (1997).

There is a significant positive relationship between the banks' process performance and financial performance for each of the financial measures as shown in Table 6. That is, as aggregate process performance improves, so does financial performance. Of course, there are two explanations for this relationship. First, it may be the case that better process performance does indeed drive financial performance.

The other explanation is that firms that are financially secure have the resources to be better process performers. In addition, there could well be other drivers of financial performance for which we need to control. To this end, we have run multivariate regressions with aggregate process performance and firm size (as measured by log assets) as the independent variables.

We use firm size since it is commonly believed to be the largest determinant of financial performance. Our results demonstrate that, for our sample of banks, while there is not a clear relation between firm size and our financial performance measures and there is a clear relation between aggregate process performance and our financial performance measures.

While these simple regressions cannot conclusively determine that aggregate process performance affects firm financial performance, this evidence does, in concert with theoretical and anecdotal evidence, suggest that aggregate process performance as we have measured it, is related to financial performance. Thus, we take this as support of the usefulness of our aggregation technique described herein, and recommend its use for those situations where there are repeat competitions amongst many competitors, but that not every competitor plays every other competitor.

CONCLUSIONS AND FUTURE RESEARCH

This note has presented a new methodology for determining a composite measure for performance given that a team or institution competes across several competitions, and for situations where not all teams compete with one another. The tournament ranking literature has been extended to allow for the situation in which one competitor wins all of the matches between two competitors. The approach was then used to illustrate how it more accurately reflects aggregate performance than such traditional measures as average performance.

The proposed methodology treats all processes as equivalent when undertaking the aggregation procedure. Obviously, some processes are more important to an organization or an industry than others. Thus, a clear extension of the current methodology is to weight the various process performance metrics by their importance, and to then conduct the synthesis to generate the institutional rankings; this is left for future research. In order to accomplish this weighting, we would need to solicit expert judgments or data on worth of the relative importance of each process using a methodology like the Analytic Hierarchy Process (Saaty 1986). We have presented the basic mechanics in our model, which is easily extended to allow for this circumstance.

3

MONETARY POLICY

INTRODUCTION

There is a long tradition in monetary economics of searching for a single policy variable perhaps a monetary aggregate, perhaps an interest rate that is more or less controlled by policy and stably related to economic activity. Whether the variable is conceived as an "indicator of policy" or a "measure of policy stance", correlations between it and macro time series are taken to reflect the effects of monetary policy. Conditions for the existence of such a variable are stringent.

Essentially policy choices must evolve autonomously, independently of economic conditions. Even the harshest critics of monetary authorities would not maintain policy decisions are unrelated to the economy. The line of work we extend builds on a venerable econometric tradition to emphasize the need to specify and estimate behavioral relationships for policy. The estimated relationships separate the regular response of policy to the economy from the response of the economy to policy, arriving at a more accurate measure of the effects of policy changes.

One sometimes encounters a presumption that models for "policy analysis" and "forecasting" are sharply distinct. A model useful for policy choice need not fit data well and well-fit models necessarily sacrifice economic interpretability. We do not share this presumption, and aim here to show that it is possible to construct economically interpretable models with superior fit to the data.

As the recent empirical literature on the effects of monetary policy has developed ways of handling more complex, multivariate data sets, a variety of models and approaches has emerged. Researchers have chosen different data sets, made different assumptions, and tended to emphasize the differences between their results and those of others, rather than the commonalities. This paper uses a single time frame and data set to test the robustness of results in this recent literature and to trace the nature and sources of differences in conclusions.

We analyze and interpret the data in ways that do not impose strong economic beliefs. The methods we employ permit estimation of large time series models, allowing more comprehensive analysis of the data. Some of the models integrate policy behavior with the banking system, the demand for a broad monetary aggregate, and a rich array of goods and financial market variables, providing a more complete understanding of the monetary transmission mechanism. Weak economic assumptions and large models combine to reveal difficulties with sorting out policy effects that other approaches fail to bring out.

The size of effects attributed to shifts in monetary policy varies across specifications of economic behavior. We show, though, that most of the specifications imply that only a modest portion (or in some cases, essentially none) of the variance of output or prices in the US since 1960 is attributable to shifts in monetary policy. Furthermore, we point out substantive problems in the models that imply large real effects, and argue that correcting these problems lowers the implied size of the real effects.

Another robust conclusion, common across these models, is that a large fraction of the variation in monetary policy instruments is attributable to systematic reaction by policy authorities to the state of the economy. This is of course what we would expect of good monetary policy, but it is also the reason why using the historical behavior of aggregate time series to uncover the effects of monetary policy is difficult.

METHOD

Our work uses a class of models, called "identified vector autoregressions", that has begun to be widely used only recently. Nonetheless a considerable part of previous empirical research on the effects of monetary policy uses methods that fit within this general framework. In this section we describe the framework itself, summarize its differences from other widely used frameworks, and consider some common criticisms of the framework. In the following section we discuss the ways we and others have put substantive meat on the abstract skeleton of a method we discuss in this section.

Model Form

We use a class of models called "identified vector autoregressions." These models break up the variation in a list of time series into mutually independent components, according to the following general scheme. Iyf (t) is a k 1 vector of time series.

where the disturbance vector e(t) is uncorrelated with y(s) for s t and has an identity covariance matrix. We assume A0 is invertible, which guarantees that we can solve (1) to produce.

The elements of Cs, treated as functions of s, are known as the model's impulse responses, as they delineate how each variable iny responds over time to each disturbance ine.

Identification

To use this mathematical structure for economic policy analysis we have to identify it, meaning we have to give its elements economic interpretations. The mathematical model explains all variation in the data as arising from the independent disturbances e. Since in this paper we are studying the effects of monetary policy, we need to specify an element of the e vector, or a list of its elements, that represents disturbances to monetary policy. The equation system (1) contains one equation for each element of the e vector, defining it as a function of current and past values of y(t). So specifying the element or elements of e that correspond to monetary policy is equivalent to specifying an equation or set of equations that characterizes monetary policy behavior.

These equations can be thought of as describing relations among current and past y's that hold exactly when there are no disturbances to policy. They are, in other words, policy rules or reaction functions. The remaining equations of the system describe the non-policy part of the economy, and their disturbances are non-policy sources of variation in the economy.

While representations of the behavior of the y time series in the form (1) and (2) exist under fairly general conditions, they are not unique. That is, models in this form with different A and (therefore) C coefficients may imply exactly the same behavior of y.

Because the implications of the model for the effects of a change in monetary policy are determined by A and C, this means that models with different policy implications may be indistinguishable on the basis of their fit to the data.

When this is true, the model is said to be unidentified. The nature of the nonuniqueness is as follows. Given any matrix W satisfying W W I, i.e. any orthonormal matrix, we can replace e by We, A(L) by WA(L), and C(L) by C(L)W, arriving at a new representation of the same form. Since the new version of the model is just a linear transformation of the old one, it implies the same time series properties for the data y.

Only if we know enough about the form of A (or, equivalently, C) to rule out some transformed WA's or CW 's as implausible or impossible will the data be able to lead us to the most likely form A o. f We use three sorts of restrictions in order to pin down the connection between A and the implied behavior of y.

That is, we use three sorts of identifying restrictions. One is exact linear restrictions on the elements of A0, usually setting certain elements to zero. If we rely entirely on these, we know that we will need at least k (k 1) 2 of them, because a k k orthonormal matrix has this many free parameters.

Once we have this number of restrictions on the elements of A0, the restriction equations, together with the k bk 1g 2 independent restrictions in the W W I requirement, are enough equations to make W unique.5 Another sort of identifying restriction is probabilistic assertions about elements of A-assertions that certain values or relations among values of elements of A are more likely than others. And the third is informal restrictions on the reasonableness of the impulse responses, the C's in (2).

The first two types are easy to handle mathematically, while the latter is difficult mathematically. It is used informally, in that we focus attention on results that do not produce implausible impulse responses. Our criterion for plausibility is loose. We do not expect to see strongly positive responses of prices, output, or monetary aggregates, or strongly negative responses of interest rates, to monetary contraction.

The fact that we use this sort of identifying information informally may give the impression that we are doing undisciplined data mining. But we could have done the same thing, at much more computational cost, by imposing our beliefs in the forms of impulse responses as precise mathematical restrictions. This would not have been any more "disciplined" than our actual procedure. Our procedure differs from what empirical researchers in economics always do only in being possibly less apologetic.

Economists adjust their models until they both fit the data and give "reasonable" results. There is nothing unscientific or dishonest about this. What would be unscientific or dishonest would be hiding results for models that fit much better than the one displayed (even if the hidden model seemed unreasonable) or for models that fit about as well as those reported and that support other interpretations of the data that some readers might regard as reasonable. We are doing nothing of this sort.

Our approach to identification here is very similar to that of the rest of the identified VAR literature, but it differs from some other approaches to quantitative macroeconomics. The differences correspond in some cases to criticisms that those taking other approaches often make of the identified VAR approach.

Comparison to Other Approaches

Traditional econometric simultaneous equations (SE) modeling works with systems quite similar in form to those we deal with. It begins with a system in the form (1), usually with our assumption that the e vector is uncorrelated across time, and always without our assumption that e has an identity covariance matrix. With an unrestricted as covariance matrix for e, the mathematical structure is subject to a wider range of transformations that leave the implications of the model for data unchanged.

While the identified VAR framework admits an arbitrary orthonormal W as a transformation matrix, the standard simultaneous equations framework admits an arbitrary non-singular matrix V in the same role. So in order to pin down the mapping between e and the data, stronger a priori restrictions on A are required in the SE approach. Traditionally these take two forms.

One form is block triangularity restrictions on contemporaneous interactions among variables (A0 from (1)) that are linked to conformable block diagonality restrictions on Ω. Such a combination of restrictions breaks the variable list into two components, one usually labeled "predetermined", the other labeled "endogenous".

The second form of traditional restriction then adds linear constraints (again, often simply setting coefficients to zero) on the elements of the rows ofA corresponding to the endogenous variables. To get a feeling for the difference in requirements for identification between identified VAR's and traditional simultaneous equations, it may help to consider the simplest possible model.

In a two-equation system with no lags, a single zero restriction on A0 suffices for identification in the identified VAR framework. That is, the system in which we have imposed the single constraint a21 0, has a unique mapping from A to the stochastic properties (here just the covariance matrix) of y.

The y vector is implied to have a covariance matrix A0A0, and A0 can be found from as its unique upper triangular square root, or Choleski decomposition. If (3) is interpreted as a traditional simultaneous equations system, however, it is not identified-arbitrary linear combinations of the two equations satisfy all the restrictions (since there are none) on the form of the first equation, while leaving the implications of the system for the behavior of y unchanged.

A nonsingular linear transformation of the system can replace the first equation by a linear combination of the two equations, while leaving the second equation unchanged. An orthonormal linear transformation must change both equations at once, in order to preserve the lack of correlation of the disturbances. This is why the system is not identified as a standard SE model, while it is identified as our type of identified VAR model.

This kind of system, called recursive, is a well-recognized special case in the simultaneous equations literature.6 In this two-variable version, a single linear restriction on any of the four coefficients in A0, together with the usual identified VAR restriction that the e's are uncorrelated, is equivalent to the traditional SE modeling assumption that one of the variables in the system is predetermined.

Impulse responses can be computed for traditional SE models as well as for identified VAR's. The restriction that in an identified VAR we have Var(e) I, though, means that in some circumstances conclusions about model behavior are less dependent on identifying assumptions on A in identified VAR's than in SE models. Consider an example that arises in our discussion below.

We might find that the rows of C(L) corresponding to prices and interest rates (the first and second rows, say) mostly show prices and interest rates moving in the same direction when they show any substantial movement-$c1_j$ (s) and $c2_j$ (s) of the same sign for most j and s when either $c1_j$ (s) or $c2_j$ (s) is large. We might expect that the response to a monetary policy shock should show the opposite sign pattern, with $c1_j$ (s) and $c2_j$ (s) moving in opposite directions. Then we can conclude that monetary policy disturbances cannot account for much of the observed variation in prices and interest rates, regardless of what identifying restrictions we may invoke. It is true that linear transformations of the system will correspond to linear transformations of the disturbances.

Some linear transformations, differences for example, of responses that have $c1_j$ (s) and $c2_j$ (s) of the same sign could easily show $c1_j$ (s) and $c2_j$ (s) of opposite signs. But orthonormal transformations of responses that all show large, same-signed movements of c1 j (s) and c2 j (s) cannot produce transformed responses that are both oppositesigned and large. In other words, if most disturbances that produce substantial responses of interest rates show substantial prices in the same direction, then it is characteristic of the data that these two variables tend to move in the same direction.

A monetary policy disturbance, which moves the two variables in opposite directions, cannot then be accounting for more than a small part of overall variance in interest rates. In a traditional SE model we could not reach the same conclusion, because we would have to admit the possibility that there could be a monetary policy shock with large variance, offset by another shock that also moves prices and interest rates in opposite directions but is negatively correlated with the monetary disturbance.

This brings out what we see as an advantage of insisting that a well-specified model accounts for all correlations among disturbances, so that they end up with an identity covariance matrix. When the historical record shows a very strong pattern of positive co-movement between interest rates and prices, then if we believe that monetary policy disturbances would generate negative comovements, it is reasonable to conclude that monetary policy disturbances have not been a major source of variation in the data. Insistence that it could be true that monetary policy disturbances were important, but that they tend to be systematically offset by private sector disturbances that occur at the same time, seems strained.

If this is the actual situation, it raises questions about the model. Do the offsetting private sector shocks occur because of an effect of monetary policy on the private sector shocks? If so, then in effect our model implies that once the full effects of a monetary policy disturbance are accounted for, it does not move interest rates and prices in opposite directions, which is suspicious. Do the offsetting shocks arise because of an effect of the private sector on policy-making? Then we ought to account for this as part of the model of policy behavior.

Objections to Identified VAR Modeling

It is sometimes suggested that disturbances are what is "omitted from the theory", and that therefore we cannot claim to know much about their properties. Note, though, that traditional predeterminedness assumptions make assertions about lack of correlation among sources of variation of just the sort made in identified VAR models. If we really know nothing about the stochastic properties of disturbance terms, we will not be able to distinguish disturbances from systematic components of variation.

Furthermore, any actual use of models for policy analysis makes correlation among disturbances a serious embarrassment. If disturbances to the monetary policy reaction function are strongly correlated with private sector disturbances, how are we to use the system to simulate the effects of variations in monetary policy?

The usual answer in practice is that simulations of the effects of paths of policy variables or of hypothetical policy rules are conducted under the assumption that such policy changes can be made without producing any change in disturbance terms in other equations, even if the estimated covariance matrix of disturbances shows strong correlations. This is not logically inconsistent, but it amounts to the claim that the true policy disturbance is that part of the reaction function residual that is not correlated with other disturbances in the system.

This in turn is equivalent to the claim that the true reaction function is a linear combination of what the model labels as the reaction function and the other equations in the system whose disturbances are correlated with it. Our view is that if one is going to do this in the end, the assumptions on the model that justify it should be explicit from the beginning.

Traditional SE modelers also sometimes find puzzling the focus on "policy shocks" in the identified VAR approach. This is largely a semantic confusion. As we have already pointed out, identifying policy shocks is equivalent to identifying equations for policy reaction functions. Also, distinguishing these shocks from other sources of disturbance to the system is equivalent to identifying the non-policy equations of the model, which determine the response of the system to policy actions or to changes in the policy rule.

The prominent role given to discussion of shocks in presentations of identified VAR results just reflects a sharp focus on the model's characteristics as a probability model of the data. In practice traditional SE approaches often focus on the equations, with the remainder of the stochastic structure treated casually. Identified VAR results are often presented as tables or charts of "responses to shocks", the C's in (2). But these carry exactly the same information about the model as the A's in (1), the "equation coefficients" that are more commonly presented in traditional SE modeling approaches.

Of course presentations of SE models also often include simulations of the model with various kinds of perturbations fed into it. The C's can be thought of as a systematic set of simulations, of responses to a range of types of disturbance wide enough to display all aspects of the model's behav.ior Another branch of quantitative macroeconomics, the dynamic stochastic general equilibrium (DSGE) approach, criticizes identified VAR modeling for resembling traditional SE modeling too closely. Traditional SE models in practice generally contain expectational terms that are modeled as linear functions of past data.

The models were sometimes used to examine the effects of making large, permanent changes in policy rules. The policy equations were replaced by possible new rules, and the model was simulated with the remaining equations, including the expectational terms, left in unchanged form. Such exercises are potentially misleading, because they contradict the probability structure of the estimated model.

The model was fit to historical data under the assumption that the historical variation in policy can be accounted for by the model's stochastic disturbances-the additive error terms in the policy reaction functions. In the simulation experiment quite a different form of variation in policy is examined. If variations in policy of this form are not historically unprecedented, there is a misspecification in the model: something the model's structure implies is impossible has actually occurred in the past.

Recognizing this contradiction should remind us of the need for caution in extrapolating model results to predictions about situations far from what has been observed historically. It is not uninteresting to try changing the policy rule equations in the model, holding the other equations fixed, so long as we recognize that the changed policy rule equations are just a convenient way of generating an interesting sequence of disturbances to the originally estimated policy rule. When the implied sequence of policy rule disturbances (i.e., policy shocks) is very different in size or serial correlation properties from what has been observed historically, the model may become unreliable.

A more common label for this approach is the "real business cycle" approach. But while this approach began with models that contained no nominal rigidities and no role for monetary policy, its methodology has now been extended to models that include nominal rigidities, for example J. Kim [1996].

The DSGE literature has, surprisingly in the light of its connection to the idea of rational expectations, largely ignored this cautionary conclusion. Actual changes in monetary policy are recognized in advance by the public as possible policy actions. Since they are recognized in advance as possibilities, yet are not known with certainty to be occurring, when they do (or don't) occur the result is that a random variable is realized. One would think it is then a central conclusion of a rational expectations approach to policy analysis that the stochastic nature of policy changes is always important to correct analysis of their effects. A starting point for rational expectations analysis of policy changes over time should be recognition that they should always be modeled as sequences of values for disturbance terms.

Yet instead, the DSGE approach has often embraced the idea that the only kinds of policy changes worth studying are changes that are historically unprecedented, occur as complete surprises to the agents populating the model, and are sure never to be reversed. If a change in the policy reaction function is of this type, DSGE models do give an internally consistent answer as to the effects of the policy change. But the need for caution is still as great as with traditional SE models.

Any evidence in the data about the effects of such an unprecedented policy shift has to be entirely indirect, an extrapolation based on a priori assumptions to a range of experience outside the range to which the model has been fit. And the results, despite being internally consistent, are answers to an uninteresting question. DSGE models as they are usually used in policy analysis describe the effects of policy changes of a type that never in fact occurs.

These days the models that have evolved from traditional SE models often trace out the effects of nonstochastic shifts in policy reaction functions using rational expectations, just as do most DSGE modelers. Though the two types of models make very different choices in the tradeoffs among model abstraction, internal consistency, and fit to the data, the inherent limitations of simulating non-stochastic shifts in policy rules are common to both DSGE and the newer SE-style models.

Note that there is a common thread in criticism of the identified VAR approach from the SE modeling side and the DSGE modeling side: both sides show discomfort with the notion of treating policy as "random". Some people have the idea that we cannot contemplate improving policy as if we could choose it rationally and at the same time think of it as a random variable.

This notion is simply incorrect. When we consider historical policy decisions, we have to recognize that policy pursues multiple objectives in an uncertain environment. Economists at the Board of Governors and Federal Reserve Banks collect and analyze a large set of economic information on which the Federal Open Market Committee bases its decisions. Committee members compare staff forecasts of a wide range of macro variables to the members' desired paths for these variables. Each member's policy choice minimizes a loss function subject to a set of ancillary constraints, such as a desire to smooth interest rates and avoid disrupting financial markets.

Federal Reserve policy is an outgrowth of both the members' economic concerns and the dynamic interplay among members. The result of this process is surely as "random" as any other aspect of economic behavior that we might try to model.

When we consider offering advice on current or future policy decisions, we of course would not ordinarily propose flipping a coin to choose policy, but this does not mean that it is a mistake to think of policy choice as the realization of a random variable. Choices that are made systematically by one person or group are likely still to be unpredictable from the perspective of others.

If, in a break with the past, monetary policy were to begin being set by a single, internally consistent, rational policy maker, this would be surprising to the public, and they would most likely remain uncertain for some time that the new pattern would persist. Even if we think of our modeling efforts as addressed to such a hypothetical unified rational policy maker, then, we would want to model policy choices as realizations of random variables in tracing their impact on the economy.

People who use models for policy analysis have generally understood DSGE-style analysis of non-stochastic changes in policy rule as characterizing effects of policy changes in the long run and understood analysis of the effects of policy shocks, with the reaction function equation fixed, as characterizing short run effects. This is a reasonable interpretation, by and large. It recognizes that, if we can realistically contemplate changing coefficients in policy reaction functions that are treated in the model as non-stochastic, this is a source of-inaccuracy in the model, requiring caution in "long run" extrapolations. It also recognizes that DSGE-style analysis of policy rule shifts, because it models policy as non-stochastic, cannot be applied to projecting the effects of policy changes of the type, and over the time horizons, that are the main subject of policy discussion.

Ideally, we would like a model without either sort of limitation, whose stochastic characterization of policy behavior encompassed shifts in policy of all the kinds we actually consider. In such a model every interesting and plausible policy change, including ones that seem naturally described as changes in policy "rule", would be expressible as a sequence of shocks to the model's driving random variables. There are a few models in the literature that go some way toward this goal, modeling policy as switching between linear rules with additive errors according to some well defined Markov process, for example. But the analytical difficulties raised by even simple models like this are substantial.

We should add that this sharp contrast between DSGE modelers' approach to analysis of policy changes and our own reflects only a difference between common practice of DSGE modelers and our own methods.

There is nothing in principle that ties DSGE models to the approach that has commonly been taken by DSGE modelers to policy analysis. Indeed Leeper and Sims [1994] and J. Kim [1996] are examples of DSGE models in which careful attention is paid to modeling the stochastic structure of policy and in which therefore the effects both of stochastic disturbances to policy and of deterministic changes in policy rule can be examined. There is also no fundamental conflict between the mathematics of our modeling approach in this paper and that of DSGE models.

Most DSGE models are of course nonlinear, whereas ours our linear, but nonlinearities in DSGE models are usually not strong. Indeed one common approach to solving and fitting DSGE models to data is to take a linear approximation to them around a steady state. A linearized DSGE model becomes a VAR model, with a particular pattern of identifying restrictions on its coefficients. Linearized DSGE models are generally much more strongly restricted than identified VAR models, so that they involve many fewer free parameters to estimate. However the kinds of restrictions that are used to identify VAR models are often imposed as a subset of the restrictions used in DSGE models, so that identified VAR models can be thought of simply as weakly restricted DSGE models.

This is what in fact distinguishes DSGE from identified VAR modeling approaches. The former begins with a complete interpretation of each source of stochastic disturbance in the model, invoking many conventional but arbitrary restrictions on functional forms of utility and production functions and on stochastic properties of disturbances.

The fitted model then has a full story to tell about how each source of disturbance affects the economy and the routes by which it does so. The identified VAR modeling approach instead begins with an unidentified time series model of the economy and introduces identifying information cautiously. The fitted model then fits the data well, usually much better than DSGE models of the same data, but has only an incomplete story to tell about how each source of disturbance affects the economy and the routes by which it does so. In an identified VAR typically many sources of disturbance are not completely interpreted, identified only as part of a vector of "private sector shocks", for example, that may mix technology shocks and taste shocks. The effects of monetary policy disturbances on the economy may be traced out, but complete stories as to how the effects work their way through the behavior of investors and consumers may not be available.

Each approach has its advantages and disadvantages. The identified VAR approach may give a more accurate impression of the true degree of uncertainty about results that emerge from the model. It also reduces the chance that we will be misled into thinking the data imply a result that actually flows almost entirely from initial ad hoc modeling assumptions. On the other hand, the identified VAR approach does not provide as convenient a framework for bringing to bear a priori knowledge or hypotheses about the structure of the economy.

Our conclusion after considering alternatives to and criticisms of the identified VAR approach is that such strictly linear, weakly identified models do have limitations. We would be uncomfortable extrapolating our estimates of policy effects to regimes of hyperinflation or to very different fiscal policy environments, for example.10 But we regard it as an advantage, not a defect, of our approach that it recognizes the stochastic nature of variation in policy.

Inference

We take the perspective of the likelihood principle in measuring model fit and assessing how well various hypotheses accord with the data. That is, we take the task of reporting efforts at statistical model-fitting to be the task of characterizing the shape of the likelihood function. Most

10 Actually, we would be equally uncomfortable extrapolating policy effects implied by DSGE models fitted or calibrated to US data to such situations. But for somewhat

different reasons. existing econometric procedures can be interpreted as reasonable from this perspective.

However it is a different perspective than what is usually taught in econometrics courses, and it does have implications that should affect practice in some areas, particularly when, as in this paper, nearnon- stationary models or models with large numbers of parameters are being considered. We do not have space here to elaborate on it, but interested readers can consult Berger and Wolpert [1988] for a general discussion of the principle and Gelman, Carlin, Stern and Rubin [1995] for an approach to applied statistical work that takes a likelihood-principle perspective.

As we discuss results below, we will not be presenting measures of model fit and testing the restrictions in the models. Such tests can be useful as part of describing the likelihood function, but the models we are dealing with are for the most part only weakly overidentified. That is, they are almost as unrestricted as an unidentified reduced form model.

Accordingly, they tend to fit very well in comparison to such models, and this is neither surprising nor very powerful evidence in favor of the interpretations of the data that they embody. We do present error bands about the impulse responses we trace out for our models.11 These are important, because often differences among models in the form of their implied responses to monetary policy shocks influence our conclusions about how reliable the models are. We would not want to be choosing among models on the basis of differences in their implied impulse responses if estimates of those responses were in fact not sharply determined.

In models as large as some of those we consider here, the likelihood function itself can be illbehaved. This is related to the well-known tendency of estimates to become unreasonable when degrees of freedom are low. We therefore multiply all the likelihood functions we discuss by a probability density function that downweights models with large coefficients on distant lags or with explosive dynamics. This p.d.f. plays the formal role of a Bayesian prior distribution, but it is not meant to represent a summary of all prior information we might have about model parameters. It is meant only to reflect, in a transparent way, beliefs that are likely to be uncontroversial across a wide range of users of the analysis. This makes it possible to discuss larger models than have been feasible with previous approaches. The details of our reference prior are described in the Appendix, and the methods we use are put in a more general context Sinim s and Zha [1996.]

IDENTIFYING MONETARY POLICY

The history of empirical work in this area is largely one of expanding model scale, with progress in understanding of models at one scale providing the basis for expansion to more complex models. Most of this history can be described in the identified VAR framework, though much of it pre-existed the codification of this framework. We also recognize that to some extent what we are describing is not an evolution over time, but a layering of evidence, using models of different levels of complexity, all of which are influencing economists beliefs even now.

The simplest level of evidence involves bivariate modeling, with some single variable taken as a measure of the stance of monetary policy. Here the usual approach has been to argue that the monetary policy measure can be taken to be predetermined.

Timing Patterns

Part of the strength of the view that monetary policy has been an important generator of business cycle fluctuations comes from certain patterns in the data, apparent to the eye, that seem to support this view. For example, most postwar US recessions have been preceded by rising interest rates. If one concludes from this that most postwar US recessions have been preceded by periods of monetary tightening, the evidence for an important role of monetary policy in generating recessions seems strong. While it can be shown that one variable's "leading" another in timing is neither a necessary nor a sufficient condition for its being predetermined in a bivariate system of the form (1), people tend to assume, probably correctly, that the two conditions are at least likely to occur together, so a graph like this influences peoples' beliefs about the effects of monetary policy.

But a little reflection turns up the problems of interpretation--identification problems in other words--that are pervasive in this area. Interest rates were generally rising from the 50's through the 70's. Interest rates fall sharply after business cycle peaks. How much of the pattern that strikes the eye comes simply from the rising trend interacting with the post-peak rate drops?

The one cyclical peak that clearly does not show a preceding rate increase is also the only one since the early 80's, i.e. the only one during a period of generally declining interest rates. Interest rates are cyclical variables. The Producers' Price Index for Crude Materials. Monetary policy, in order to control inflation, needs to set interest rates systematically, reacting to the state of the economy. If it does so, then whether or not it influences the state of real activity.

In what might be regarded as an early real business cycle model, Tobin [1970] showed that the timing patterns that monetarists had been documenting in order to support models with a causal role for monetary policy in generating cycles could emerge instead in a model with no such role for monetary policy. He answered the rich array of informally interpreted time series evidence presented by Milton Friedman and other monetarists with a simple dynamic general equilibrium model showing an alternative interpretation of essentially the same facts. Though both the analysis of the empirical evidence and the theoretical models have grown more complex, the pattern of interplay between data and models today still echoes the Friedman-Tobin debate in many respects.

The recent literature has studied the joint behavior of larger sets of relevant time series. It has begun to explore the gap between text book macro models-with a single "M" and a single "R"- and the real world of monetary policy, with multiple definitions of M, reserves borrowed and unborrowed, and multiple interest rates. The counterarguments are now based on stochastic, rather than deterministic, dynamic general equilibrium models and are aimed at accounting for more than the simple timing relationships Tobin addressed.

Money and Income, Post Hoc Ergo Propter Hoc, Redux

Though the monetarist policy view is out of fashion, the statistical time series regularities that made it plausible are still there. The monetarist interpretation of them retains its surface appeal, and it remains an important test of other policy views that they be able to explain these regularities. Surprise changes in the stock of money ("innovations" in M) are persistent and predict subsequent movements in both prices and output in the same direction.

As Milton Friedman argued, this relationship is more than a correlation and a timing pattern. The timing of cyclical peaks is notoriously sensitive to differencing or other filtering of the data. The fact that monetary aggregates contain substantial variation that past output data does not help predict, and that this variation in M does help predict future output,-is invariant to data filtering. The response-of the price level to an M innovation is smooth and slow; the response of output is quicker and less sustained. Innovations in prices and output have little predictive power for money.

The VAR system, like all those displayed in this paper, was estimated by finding the posterior mode using the reference prior described in the Appendix. Impulse responses in this reduced form were orthogonalized recursively in the order shown in the figure, with the last listed variable's innovation untransformed, the second to last taken as the part orthogonal to the last, etc. There were 6 lags and a constant term in the system.

The responses are shown over 48 months. Data are measured in log units, except for interest rates, which are measured as annual rates (not per cent). Error bands represent 68% probability bands, point by point (approximately one-standard-error bands, if the posterior p.d.f. had a jointly Normal shape.) stated we will be using the 1960:1 through 1996:3 time period as the estimation period, with six lags (so that the first data used are in 1959:7), and will be measuring all variables in log units except for interest rates and the unemployment rate.

The smooth, slow response of prices does not easily fit a rational expectations monetarist view that treats money stock surprises as equivalent to price surprises. The money surprise leads to very predictable inflation, later. But a more eclectic monetarist view, that holds that money's effects arise through a variety of temporary frictions and money illusion, but that they dissipate over time. Note, though, that the each row of graphs is all on a common scale, so that the three responses displayed in the middle row "add up" (in a mean square sense) to an explanation for all the variation in output. The proportion accounted for by money surprises is small.

Furthermore, the error bands show that versions of the model with no response at all of real output to money surprises are not strongly inconsistent with the data. (They seem to be within a "two-standarderror" band.) This model is therefore not consistent with the view that most business cycle fluctuations arise from random fluctuations in monetary policy. Though not often emphasized, the weakness of the statistical relation between monetary aggregates and real activity was noted even in early studies that used careful time series methods16, and has been reconfirmed recently by B. Friedman and Kuttner [1992].

Interest Rates

In Sims [1980] one of us pointed out that though little of the variation in monetary aggregates is predictable from data on past prices and output, a considerable amount is predictable once information on past interest rates is taken into account. The component of money variation that is predictable from interest rates is more strongly related to output changes than other components.

The proportion of output variation attributable to money stock surprises drops substantially in a system that includes a short interest rate. This pattern is confirmed in Figure 4, which shows that in a system including an interest rate on federal funds, money innovations have lost much of their predictive power for output.

The responses to money innovations in this system show what is sometimes called the "liquidity puzzle": the interest rate declines only very slightly and temporarily as M jumps upward.18 Central bankers usually think of themselves as controlling monetary aggregates via their control of interest rates, with lower interest rates inevitably accompanying a policygenerated expansion of M. The estimated pattern of response to a money innovation,-with little or no reduction of interest rates as M rises, therefore seems to contradict common sense. The liquidity effect, which hypothesizes that the policy-induced increased liquidity of a monetary expansion should lower interest rates, seems not to be present.

This is not a problem for the interest rate innovation, corresponding to the third column of the figure. If this column is interpreted as representing a monetary contraction, it shows a strong liquidity effect, with money contracting quickly and staying persistently lower than average following an interest rate jump that is itself persistent. After an initial delay of six months or so, output declines persistently.

But here we encounter what has been labeled the "price puzzle." In the first row of the third column, we see that prices rise steadily following an interest rate innovation. Interpreting column 3 as a monetary contraction therefore requires accepting that monetary contraction produces inflation, which seems as unlikely an idea as the notion that monetary expansion fails to lower interest rates.

Notice that, though the fourth column displays a liquidity puzzle if it is the monetary policy shock, and the third column displays a price puzzle, it looks like the puzzles might be eliminated by taking something close to a difference of the two columns. The third column minus the fourth would show a positive movement in the Funds Rate, less persistent than that in column 3, a negative movement in M1 more pronounced than in either column separately, a negative movement in Y without as much of an initial positive blip as in column 3 but with less persistence, and little movement in P. It turns out that a set of restrictions on A0 that in itself has some appeal delivers approximately this result. We present this very small model not as a preferred interpretation of the data, but as an illustration of types of reasoning and interpretation that we will apply again in more complicated settings below.

Suppose we postulate that, because data on the price level and output emerge only from complex data-gathering and processing that takes time, monetary policy makers do not respond within the month to changes in P and Y. Suppose further that we assume that P and Y are unresponsive within the month to changes in R and M. The justification for this assumption is that there are planning processes involved in changing output or in changing the prices of final goods.

This is not to say that P and Y show no short-run changes. Crop failures, new inventions, consumers turning out to hate the new fall line of coats-can result in short-run variation in P and Y. But the financial signals embodied in monetary variables are postulated to influence P and Y only smoothly over time, very little within a month. This set of restrictions can be displayed in a matrix of X's and blanks.

The X's indicate coefficients in A0 that are unrestricted, the blanks coefficients that are postulated to be zero. The labels in the first row are variable names. The bold labels in the first column are names of disturbances or shocks. The F shock is meant to represent random variation in Federal Reserve behavior, the P shocks private behavior of inertial variables that do not respond quickly to financial signals, and the I shock other disturbances to private sector behavior. (The I stands for "information", meaning that this component of non-policy behavior responds quickly to new information.)

The two P equations have the same restrictions, and are therefore 19 We could have labeled this equation "Md", fo money demand, as it contains contemporaneously all four of the traditional arguments of liquidity preference in an ISLM -model.

However over much of our sample period most of the deposits that make up M1 paid interest, so a short interest rate like Rf did not represent the opportunity cost of holding M1. Probably more importantly, in this small model this sector has to be the locus of all non-policy effects on the indistinguishable. They can be premultiplied by any orthonormal 2x2 matrix and still satisfy the same restrictions. Since we do not have separate interpretations for these two equations, we normalize them arbitrarily by changing the Y coefficient in the first row from an X to a blank. This results in a system that is overidentified by one restriction.

The fourth column of this Figure is a plausible candidate as a measure of the effect of a tightening of monetary policy. Rf rises initially, then returns to its original level over the course of a year or so. M1 declines, and most of the variation in M1 is accounted for by these policy disturbances. Y declines, persistently, but not much of the overall variance in output is attributed to the policy disturbance. P moves negligibly-very slightly downward.

There are some problems with the interpretation. Since the output decline is so small (only about a tenth of a per cent), the price decline negligible, and the interest rate increase so temporary, it is hard to understand why M1 responds so strongly and persistently (by almost a full percentage point). interest rate and M1. Thus we would not want to insist that this equation must be interpreted as money demand.

Note that the first three columns show that every private sector shock that implies inflation engenders a contractionary response in the interest rate. As we observed earlier, in discussing the robustness of conclusions from identified VAR's, this assures us that certain aspects of the results are not sensitive to the identifying assumptions. Most of observed variation in the interest rate is accounted for by these endogenous responses, not by what have been identified as policy shocks.

Most variation in output and prices is accounted for by the first and third columns, which look like "supply shocks', in that they move prices and output in opposite directions, and the response of interest rates to the inflationary shock is at least as strong in these cases as when output moves in the same direction as prices.

Though this model is simple, the basic approach it takes, excluding certain variables from a contemporaneous impact on policy behavior while asserting that certain private sector variables respond only with a delay to financial variables, has been followed in one form or another in the identified VAR literature since at least Sims. Nonetheless this model cannot be a stopping place in our analysis.

Forecasters find an array of additional variables-stock prices, long interest rates, exchange rates, commodity price indexes, for example-useful in forecasting prices and output. Federal Reserve behavior could certainly depend on such indicators of the state of the economy, and by omitting such variables we relegate their effects to the disturbance term. M1 responds quickly to private sector behavior and is not directly controlled in the short run by the Federal Reserve. Bank reserves are subject to more direct control, and we have not modeled the link between them and M.

Reserves

One approach to circumventing the fact that much variation in M1 is demand-determined is simply to replace M with a reserve aggregate that the Federal Reserve could be argued to control more directly. Familiarity with textbook discussions of the money multiplier might lead one to think that this will not qualitatively change results. But this is not the case.

The output response to an M shock, already modest in 20 We discovered in the course of our work that "adjustment for reserve requirements" has dubious effects on the reserve series. Because of the way the series is constructed, the ratio of adjusted to unadjusted reserves varies substantially from month to month even in periods when no changes in reserve requirements have occurred, because of fluctuations in the distribution of deposits across categories with different reserve requirements.

This creates a component of demand-determined fluctuations in "reserves" that has nothing to do with Fed actions to change the volume of reserves. In our modeling, we sometimes found that even the signs of responses of adjusted and unadjusted reserves would differ, and that unadjusted reserves seemed to have a stronger relation to other nominal variables than adjusted reserves. Of course unadjusted reserves shows occasional large jumps, when requirements change and the change is accommodated by the Fed, that do not have the same effects as reserve changes not accompanied by requirements

Almost completely disappeared, and the price response is also much weaker. It is possible that this result is taking us closer to the truth: Use of M1 or M2 leads us to confuse endogenous components of the M aggregate with policy disturbances, exaggerating the effects of policy. However, we will see below that it is equally possible to maintain that reserves contain a substantial demand-determined component, so that neither surprise changes in reserves nor surprise changes in M are good measures of monetary policy.

Triangular System: P, Y, and TR Strongin [1995], Christiano, Eichenbaum and Evans [1996], and Bernanke and Mihov [1995] introduce some details of the banking system to analyze the consequences of the Fed's choice of the division of total reserves between borrowed and nonborrowed reserves.

By concentrating exclusively on the reserves market, omitting consumer-level monetary aggregates from the model entirely, this line of work downplays the importance of private sector money demand behavior. These models have also tended to assume a recursive economic structure, with production sector variables appearing first in the recursive orde ·ng. In addition, the authors have typically not discussed thoroughly the restrictions on nonpolicy equations that are necessary to justify their changes.

Interpretations

Bernanke and Mihov address this shortcoming by providing economic interpretations for the banking sector equations in Strongin's and Christiano, Eichenbaum, and Evans's models.21 These interpretations involve imposing restrictions not imposed by the original authors.

These reserves models can be understood in the context of a six-variable system including output, the price level, commodity prices (Pcm), the federal funds rate (Rf), nonborrowed reserves (NBR), and total reserves (TR).22 The exclusion of the discount rate is justified by regarding it as an administered rate that is infrequently changed, does not play an important role in month-to-month policy decisions, and is changed mainly as a delayed response to already existing information.

Table describes the models in terms of their A0 matrices. Equations are grouped into sectors, with a nonempty cell indicating that the variable labeled at the top of the matrix enters that equation. Empty cells correspond to zero restrictions. In the table, a "C" entry denotes a coefficient that is nonzero across models, while the "X" coefficients may or not be nonzero in different specifications. There are four behaviorally distinct sectors in the model: production (P), information (I), policy (F), and the banking system (B). Behavior in the production and information sectors is not specified, so shocks associated with those equations have no clear economic meaning other than that they are disturbances not associated with monetary policy or banking behavior.

The six-variable system allows at most 21 coefficients to be freely estimated. With the first three columns taking up 15 coefficients, no more than six unrestricted coefficients in the (3 x 3) "X" matrix may be estimated. Production and information sector variables enter policy and banking sector equations, implying those sectors observe and respond to output, overall prices, and commodity prices contemporaneously.

Variables like commodity prices, which are determined in auction markets, are observable continuously, so it may be reasonable to assume the Fed responds to information gleaned from such series. The assumption that the Fed knows current values of real GDP and consumer prices is at best an approximation to the Fed's actual information set.

Bernanke and Mihov reinterpret Strongin's and Christiano, Eichenbaum, and Evans's work by attaching behavioral meaning to each equation in the F and B sectors. They impose the restriction that the coefficients on TR and NBR in the fifth equation are equal but have opposite signs, reflecting a view that the demand for borrowed reserves, BWR, should be homogeneous in the overall level of reserves. (Particularly in the short run, as here, there is certainly no reason this has to be true, though it may be a reasonable working hypothesis.) The inclusion of Y and P in the relation follows from the fact that the demand for reserves is derived from the need to satisfy reserve requirements and the desire to manage reserve positions closely. The presence of Pc is more difficult to justify, particularly since there are many other variables that could more appropriately be included in the derived demand function.

Strongin imposes three additional restrictions. He assumes the demand for TR is interest inelastic and that the Fed sets the supply of NBR without regard to the current funds rate. Since he does not impose the equal-and-opposite-signed restriction on the NBR and TR coefficients in the second equation, his system has one overidentifying restriction.

The monetary policy shock, then, is a change in the composition between borrowed and nonborrowed reserves of a given quantity of total reserves. His model of reserves market behavior, normalized to have 1's on the diagonal, appears in Table3. Note that Strongin's work did not use theP c variable. Strongin justifies the assumption that demand is interest inelastic by appealing to institutional rigidities. He argues that within a reserve maintenance period the banking system as a whole must borrow at the discount window to meet a reserve shortfall.

With the demand for required reserves largely determined by current and past deposits, if the demand for excess reserves is unresponsive to policy, the quantity of total reserves will be determined in the short run entirely by demand.23 Though persuasive at the high frequencies associated with reserve settlement period, the argument carries less force at the monthly frequency of the data Strongin employs. Figure 7 shows the relation of excess reserves to monthly changes in required reserves over our

23 In terms of the estimated VAR, the entire monthly innovation in total reserves is attributed to shifts in the demand function. A necessary condition for the elasticity restriction to hold is that the demand for excess reserves be completely unresponsive to any variables policy may affect immediately..

sample period. Though there are more reserves relative to the monthly changes in the early and late parts of the sample, through the whole period the changes and the excess reserves are of the same order of magnitude. Banks therefore have substantial room to trade tighter management of reserves against the interest costs of carrying excess reserves. In fact simple regressions of excess reserves on interest rates suggest a substantial interest-elasticity of excess reserves.

The restriction in Strongin's identification that is most important in making his conclusions differ from those of other researchers is the claim that Federal Reserve behavior pays no attention within the month to the current Federal Funds rate. Most observers think that instead the Fed has target values of the funds rate and undertakes open market operations to stay close to those targets on a time scale considerably shorter than one month. Furthermore, Strongin assumes that the Federal Reserve manipulates the Federal Funds rate via manipulation of borrowings. In fact, most banks in most reserve accounting periods are not borrowing from the discount window at all.

This is not just because the Federal Reserve "frowns" on excessive borrowing, but also because discount-window borrowing may be regarded as a signal of possible distress or mismanagement. The Federal Funds market is a private market in which credit-worthiness of borrowers is an important concern. An individual bank that needs to borrow an unusually large amount relative to its assets or to its history of borrowings is likely to raise questions and thus in effect to face an individual upward-sloping supply of funds, just as is usually posited for individual business borrowers from banks. The Federal Reserve discount window, on the other hand, is meant to provide a safety valve for banks that are in temporary difficulties. But just because it does have this function, the fact that a bank is borrowing at the discount window may convey information, and banks may therefore be reluctant to use the discount window, despite the apparent profitability of doing so at a quoted discount rate.

Thus, though borrowing may indeed vary systematically with the structure of rates, we believe it is a mistake to think of the Fed as setting the Funds Rate by manipulating the level of borrowing. The Fed more likely sets the Funds Rate at a level it determines by assessing the overall state of the economy, undertaking open market operations to achieve its Funds Rate targets. Unusually high need for discountwindow borrowing by banks is not likely simply to be choked off by a rise in the Funds Rate, as Strongin's specification would imply. Instead the Fed is likely to maintain its Funds Rate target while accommodating a temporary rise in demand for borrowing.

Christiano, Eichenbaum and Evans [1996] assume the Fed sets the supply of NBR without regard to either TR or Rf, but relax Strongin's assumption that borrowed and non-borrowed reserves are unresponsive to the funds rate.

The rationale that Christiano, Eichenbaum, and Evans offer for their identification of policy is that open market operations directly affect non-borrowed reserves, making NBR a control variable for the monetary authority. Of course, as we have already discussed, the fact that the policy authority is choosing a variable does not imply that they do not choose to make it respond to other variables. Because this specification, like Strongin's, assumes the Fed pays no attention within the month to the Funds Rate, our arguments against Strongin's specification apply here as well.

In previous work, one of us (Sims [1992]) noted that a price puzzle, in which interest rate rises are followed by inflation, might arise in a model that did not include a rich enough specification of the information available to policy makers. If they can observe variables that forecast inflation, and if those variables are not included in the model, then there will be apparently unpredictable changes in interest rates that are actually systematic responses to information that implies inflation is on the way.

This could make it appear that tightening of monetary policy generates inflation. Christiano, Eichenbaum, and Evans introduce commodity prices to reduce this source of bias. Policy authorities are assumed to observe and react to current values of commodity prices. However, CEE merge commodity prices with other variables in the P sector, having it share with other variables in that sector the property that it has no within-month response to monetary policy variables. Since commodity prices are determined in thick auction markets and change daily, the restriction that Pcm not respond within the month to monetary policy seems strained.

Results from Two Models Using Reserves

Under Strongin's behavioral assumptions, an expansionary policy shock increases NBR and decreases BWR by exactly the same amount. Inelastic demand for reserves forces the entire adjustment to a new mix of NBR and BWR, for a given quantity of TR, to fall on the funds rate. With only the funds rate free to equilibrate supply and demand for NBR, Strongin's policy effects resemble in exaggerated form the responses to an interest rate innovation reported in Sims[1986] and Bernanke and Blinder [1992].

Strongin's Five-Variable Recursive Model

Figure 8 reports the dynamic responses over four years to shocks identified by Strongin's model.[25] The first column reports responses to a contractionary monetary policy disturbance. TR and Rf move in opposite directions, with the liquidity effect very persistent. Borrowings rise temporarily after the shock. Real GDP decreases dramatically. Prices rise smoothly and steadily. The policy shock accounts for about half the variability of output over horizons of three or more years, the majority of the fluctuations in BWR, and a substantial proportion of funds rate movements in the short run. A shock to demand for reserves shown in the second column is accommodated almost dollar-for-dollar by open market purchases that raise NBR and alleviate the need for banks to borrow at the discount window. This highlights the strong implication of Strongin's model that the entire positive contemporaneous correlation between total reserves and nonborrowed reserves gets interpreted as an endogenous response of policy to a banking sector disturbance.

The figure again confirms a feature of policy behavior that we have already encountered: monetary policy responds to shocks that portend higher prices by contracting reserves and raising the funds rate. This pattern holds even for the first P shock, which lowers output while it raises prices.

The substantial and sustained increase in prices following what is identified as a contractionary monetary policy shock in this specification confirms our view that it involves unreasonable characterizations of policy behavior that lead to confounding inflationary adverse supply disturbances originating in the private sector with what are supposed to be monetary policy disturbances.

Christiano, Eichenbaum, and Evans (CEE) add commodity prices to Strongin's five variables and relax

Strongin's assumption that a monetary policy shock only changes the mix of a fixed quantity of total reserves. By allowing some of the effect of an increase in the supply of NBR to show up in an increase in the equilibrium quantity of TR, CEE's identification moderates the large policy effects that Strongin finds.

Christiano, Eichenbaum and Evans Recursive Identification

Total reserves rise with the expansion in nonborrowed reserves, allowing borrowed reserves to fall less than dollarfor- dollar with nonborrowed reserves. Output continues to rise persistently, but policy shocks account for only a small fraction of output's variability. The price level no longer falls following a monetary expansion; in fact monetary policy shocks have essentially no effect on finished goods prices. Commodity prices, on the other hand, respond to a policy shock as one would expect, with a contractionary shock decreasing commodity prices as it raises interest rates.

The response of policy to information about future inflation is as strong here as in the other specifications we have examined. The third column of Figure 9 shows that a jump in commodity prices signaling a gradual and smoothly increasing price level induces a smooth tightening of reserves and increase in the funds rate. The endogenous response of policy to production, information, and banking sector disturbances is the dominant source of funds rate variability; policy shocks account for only a small proportion of the error variance in the funds rate. The CEE model has produced estimates of the effects of policy disturbances that are in themselves believable. However these estimates are built on assumptions about policy behavior and about the reaction of the economy to monetary policy that seem implausible.

AN INTEGRATED APPROACH

The existing research we have surveyed here has probably treated inclusion of reserves or M as mutually exclusive alternatives because of the technical and conceptual problems of working with models larger than the 6 or 7 variables included in most models in the literature. We consider in this section models that include both types of monetary aggregate, hoping to gain insight into how bank behavior and Federal Reserve policy interact.

Modeling Federal Reserve and Banking System Behavior

It is appealing to think that by using data on variables directly controlled by the Federal Reserve (like reserves, the Federal Funds Rate, and the Federal Reserve Discount Rate), together with others that are of more direct concern to banks (like Bank Loans, M2, M1, a bank loan rate index, a deposit rate index), we might come up with restrictions on which variables have an immediate impact on whose behavior, thereby separating banking system from Fed behavior.

However this is not like separating component sectors of the private economy, or supply and demand in some market. Instead of two collections of individually negligible agents as in a competitive supply and demand model, we have one such collection (banks) and another single agent (the Federal Reserve) that is concerned with regulating the banks. Data on most aspects of bank behavior and balance sheet conditions is collected regularly and with little delay by the Federal Reserve as part of its regulatory function.

We therefore do not aim at separate blocks of equations to model Federal Reserve behavior and banking system behavior. Instead we distinguish two aspects of Fed behavior:

macroeconomic policy behavior and bank regulatory behavior.

The macroeconomic aspect represents the Fed's responsibility for controlling inflation and its concern for its effects on the overall level of economic activity. The bank regulatory aspect represents its concern that the banking system function smoothly and efficiently. In the day-to-day operation of the Federal Reserve open market desk keeping track of the level of reserves and of deposit flows that generate changes in reserve requirements is a central concern, as is of course also the Federal Funds rate.

A candidate for a Federal Reserve behavior equation might seem then necessarily to include at a minimum a reserve variable and the Federal Funds rate. But in our view the Federal Reserve is concerned with reserve and deposit flows in the short run mainly because of their potential impact on the Funds rate, for which the Fed sets its objectives mainly in the light of broader macroeconomic conditions.

It tracks shifts in reserve requirements in order to accommodate them, so that they will not disturb credit markets and generate unwanted short-run macroeconomic impacts. We aim at defining one equation or block of equations that reflects how the Fed sets its desired level of interest rates in relation to the state of the economy as a whole, because a positive funds rate innovation lowers NBR, but raises TR slightly, implying that BWR do not increase dollar-for-dollar with the decline iNn BR.

While another equation or block of equations represents the joint behavior of the banking sector and the Fed in relating reserves to deposit flows. We model the Fed's behavior as not depending directly, within the month, on final goods prices, output, or GDP components, on the grounds that these variables can be measured only with substantial delay. In principle; we regard it as reasonable to allow Fed behavior to depend within the month on financial market variables that might serve as indicators of the state of the economy and that are observable on a daily basis-for example the value of the dollar, a stock price index, long interest rates, and a commodity price index.

However, there is an argument for imposing a lag on the effects of even these variables on policy. Significant shifts in the Federal Reserve's macroeconomic policy stance require a process of consultation, analysis, and consensus-building that takes time. We have considered specifications with currently observable financial variables in the Federal Reserve's reaction function contemporaneously, and also specifications without inclusion of such variables.

Allowing for possible response of monetary policy to market interest rates raises some difficulties. To understand them it may help to consider a very simple model. Suppose policy sets a one-period interest rate r(t), responding to an indicator x(t) of the state of the economy, plus a random disturbance e(t). There is a continuously observable two-period interest rate R(t) which is related to r(t) by term-structure considerations. There is also, however, a component n(t) of the spread between the two rates that is a time-varying term premium, taken in this simple example to be independent of e.

Formally, we are supposing policy:

$r(t)\ a_0x(t)\ a_1x(t_1)\ gR(t)e(t)$ (4)

arbitrage: $R(t)\ 1\ r(t)\ E_t\ r(t)\ (t)\ 2\ (1)\ n.$ (5)

To complete the system we need to specify the time series properties of x and n. We will assume n serially independent andx autoregressive according to:

x(t) qx(t 1) x(t). (6)

This points to an inherent drawback of monetary policy that reacts systematically to market interest rates. Markets depend on policy to fix a path for nominal interest rates. A policy authority too sensitive to market rates can create indeterminacy by essentially abandoning its role in anchoring the term structure. In this model it seems easy to avoid such difficulties, since the g 1 condition is simple and understandable. But if the policy authority were responding to several rates, and to other auction-market prices that are sensitive to interest rates, it might not be so clear when the boundary of indeterminacy was being crossed. If all we know about the policy reaction function is that it has the form (4), we have an identification problem.

Any linear transformation of the pair of equations (9) and (10) that gives the disturbances in the two equations an identity covariance matrix will result in a system that satisfies the basic restrictions for an identified VAR, but in which both equations have the form (4)-a linear equation in r(t), R(t), x(t), and x(t 1).

There will be versions of the system in which one equation has a scalar multiple of e as a disturbance, but also versions in which one equation has a scalar multiple of n as the disturbance. If these two equations were part of a larger model, we might have allowed for other variables to enter the equations, restricted the way they entered the two equations, and thought on this basis that we had identified the two equations. But if in fact the other variables were not important, we would have an unidentified, or weakly identified model. We would then run the risk of labeling an arbitrage condition as a policy rule and of confusing fluctuations in term risk premia with policy disturbances.

As we have set this model out, it is hard to see why the policy authority should want to react to R. We have assumed the authority can observe and react to the state of the economy, x, as rapidly as asset markets. All that the authority accomplishes by reacting to R is to make r depend on the term risk premium n in addition to x(t) and x(t 1). In these circumstances, with R containing no important information that the policy authority cannot access directly, it seems unlikely that the authority would react to R. Furthermore, even if it did react to R, we would not make a large error by estimating the model as if it did not. If we constrained the policy reaction function not to contain R, we would emerge with estimates of (9) instead of (4).

The disturbance term in (9), though, is likely to be almost the same as that in (4). It is reasonable to think that policy-generated month-to-month variation in the short rate is substantially larger than month-tomonth variation in the term risk premium.28 Thus, since y and g are both less than one, the error term in (9) is dominated by variation in e. Even if by constraining g to zero in (4) we mistakenly estimate (9) instead of (4), in other words, we will come pretty close to recovering the actual policy disturbance process, and thus also close to recovering the policy reaction function. 28 Though this is quite plausible when we are considering the "long" rate to be that on, say, a 3-month Treasury Bill and the short rate to be that on Federal Funds, it may become more dubious when we think of the long rate as that on a 10-year Treasury Bond.

The policy authority would have stronger reason to make g non-zero if it had an information disadvantage, i.e. if it was constrained to keep a0 0 in (4). Then, by reacting to R the authority could in effect make r(t) sensitive to x(t) despite its inability to observe current x directly. However in these circumstances imposing the constraint thagt 0 will firmly identify the system. This discussion suggests that we should be on the lookout for identification problems when trying to model several interest rates jointly. It makes sense to experiment with identification schemes that allow policy reactions to several longer interest rates and exclude current policy reactions to variables that are observed only with a delay. But it may turn out that such identification schemes fail, unable to distinguish between policy equations and arbitrage conditions. In that case, we may get good results by allowing only a single interest rate contemporaneously in the policy reaction function.

Notice that the criterion for whether we should include interest rates in the reaction function is definitely not the degree to which they improve the fit of a least squares regression. In this simple model, including current R on the right-hand side in a least squares estimate of a policy reaction function will generally improve the fit, and indeed will produce an estimate of that linear combination of (9) and (10) which has disturbance orthogonal to the disturbance in (10).

If, as is to be expected, n is small, this will be approximately an estimate of the arbitrage relationship, almost unrelated to the policy reaction function. Clearly a multivariate approach, with careful thinking about simultaneity, is important in avoiding serious error in this context. Through much of our sample period the behavior of one or more monetary aggregates was a focus of attention, and our models all include at least one monetary aggregate in the Fed macroeconomic policy equation. Of course an M will also appear in the equations describing the determination of reserves by joint bank and Fed behavior, representing the impact of deposit flows on required reserves.

As in our previous specifications of small models, there is a block we label P that sets "sluggish" private sector variables that do not respond immediately to financial signals. There is also a block labeled I of private sector variables that are set in auction markets and that we allow to depend contemporaneously on everything in the system. Before discussing further issues in model specification, we should look at the two sets of exclusion restrictions on A0 for which we will present estimates.

Table displays the identification scheme for the smaller model. The list of variables in the model includes both a consumer-level monetary aggregate (M1) and total reserves (TR). It also contains the unemployment rate (U), consumption (C) and both residential and non-residential investment (IR and INR), allowing us to assess the plausibility of responses to monetary policy disturbances in some detail. It avoids the complications of allowing multiple short rates into the same model by including only one, the three-month Treasury Bill rate R3.

It includes four "information variables" that are observed without delay and might influence Federal Reserve behavior: the S&P 500 stock price index (S), the 10-year Treasury Bond rate (R10), a commodity price index (Pcm) and an index of the value of the dollar (Dol).

The rows and columns of the table correspond to rows and columns of A0. The ones indicate coefficients that have been left free. The fractional entries (all.3 in this table) indicate coefficients that have been given smaller prior standard deviations than the coefficients corresponding to 1's. These entries can be thought of as "soft zero restrictions". The model was initially estimated with the prior covariance matrix determined (see the Appendix for just how) by the matrix in Table.

However, in both this model and the larger one discussed below we found that the shape of the likelihood was highly non-Gaussian when the soft zero restrictions were used, and this created numerical difficulties in constructing confidence bands for the impulse responses.

When we replaced the soft zeros with hard zeros, the non-Gaussianity diminished greatly, without greatly changing the 29 We generated error bands by simulation methods, so it may not be clear why a non- Gaussian shape causes us difficulty. We used importance sampling methods, which require that one be able efficiently to generate random draws from a reasonably good approximation to the actual p.d.f. one is studying.

With the soft zeros, the likelihood has multiple peaks and non-linear ridges, very non-Gaussian characteristics. Gaussian approximations to this form were so bad that importance sampling was prohibitively inefficient, and we did not have time to program special methods for the particular shapes we were encountering. We should note that, though we found multiple peaks, these tended either to have qualitatively similar impulse responses or to have much lower likelihood than the ones we summarize here with impulse responses.

Estimated Impulse Responses

So the results we present are those for a model with zeros in all positions where the entry inT able 5 is less than one.

Note that it labels its first two equations FB, combining banking and Fed behavior and normalizing them by setting the A0 cocfficicnt of R3 in the second equation to zero. (It turns out that the estimated coefficient on R3 in that equation is close to zero in any case, so that results are almost identical if instead the coefficient on TR in the first equation is set to zero, which might be more natural if the first equation is to be interpreted as reflecting macroeconomic policy concerns.)

In this specification the Fed is modeled as not responding contemporaneously even to available information, like Pcm or R10. Results are almost unchanged in a version of the model where Pcm is allowed in to the first two equations contemporaneously. The P block is a standard list of non-financial private sector variables, except that it includes.

In this model, consumer-level demand for M1 is taken to be interest-insensitive within the month; M1 is a private-sector sluggish variable like P and Y. This specification is not one we want to defend as necessarily correct; we have experimented with it as a working hypothesis. Results are almost completely unchanged if, while excluding Pcm, we allow R3 to enter all equations of the P block, as would be appropriate if there were a traditional money demand equation in the system, involving R3, M1, P, and Y contemporaneously, and if the disturbances in that equation were correlated with other shocks to the P sector. Then the triangularizing orthogonalization of the P block that we have imposed would spread R3 coefficients over the whole block, even if only the money demand actually contained.

The I sector relates the four information variables to all the other variables, without delay.. The sluggish sector P is allowed to depend contemporaneously on Pcm, on the grounds that one aspect of sluggish behavior, price markup rules, might create such a direct dependence. Besides the variations on this specification that we have already mentioned as leaving results unaffected (changing triangular ordering in the first two equations, allowing Pcm into the FB equations, replacing P block dependence on Pcm with dependence on R3), there are two others. We can allow U into the FB block equations, and we can exclude both Pcm and R3 from the P block equations.

The pattern of responses to the first two shocks is largely unchanged if we replace TR, which is total reserves adjusted for reserve requirements, by TRU, which is not adjusted for reserve requirement changes. The sixth column does show less tendency to oscillatory responses when TRU replaces TR, however. There are also variations that substantially change the pattern of results, and we will discuss these below, after we discuss the results themselves.

Figure 10's first column, which according to the motivation for our scheme of restrictions on A0 ought to reflect disturbances to Fed macroeconomic policy concerns, shows effects on the economy that fit its interpretation as a monetary contraction. Short and long interest rates rise; reserves and M fall smoothly; output falls and unemployment rises; GDP components fall; commodity prices drop smoothly; the value of the dollar jumps upward and then rises further, smoothly. An expanded view of this first column, with error bands.

The error bands are 68% probability bands, roughly one-standard-error on either side of the impulse response. It can be seen that most of the responses are rather sharply estimated. The response, though very small, appears to be more than two standard deviations away from zero in the positive direction for a few months. It does turn negative eventually, however, and the commodity price response is negative at all dates and roughly two standard deviations away from zero over much of the four-year span of the response.

The second column shows why a model using reserves as single monetary aggregate can be treacherous: it appears to reflect accommodation by the Fed of shifts in demand for reserves that are unrelated to movements in M1. (This result does not change notably when TRU replaces TR.) Such variation in reserves is, perhaps surprisingly, not primarily variation in excess reserves. Required reserves move quite closely in line with total reserves. The variation apparently arises from shifts in the composition of deposits among categories with different reserve requirements. We have not tried in this model to separate money demand disturbances from other P sector disturbances, and this column, because it shows a rise in P, does not look like a pure money demand shock, even though the combination of rising monetary aggregates and rising interest rates with no accompanying rise in output could arise from a shift in money demand.

Regardless of exactly how it originates, it is clear that the column-3 disturbance is the most important single source of variation in both M1 and TR and that there is nothing in its estimated form to indicate that the model's allocation of it to the P sector is an error. This is a disturbance that expands money supply and raises interest rates, without affecting output. It seems unlikely that it mistakenly incorporates much of an expansionary monetary policy disturbance. The fact that the model is led by the data to allocate so much variation in monetary aggregates to nonpolicy disturbances shows why use of monetary aggregates as one-dimensional policy indicators is unsatisfactory.

If we examine the P, Y, and U rows, we see that in each case the first two columns, corresponding to monetary policy and banking system disturbances, account for only a modest part of overall variation. For P, in fact, the first two columns make a negligible contribution. This model will not admit an interpretation of the sample period as one in which erratic shifts in monetary policy were the prime source of recessions and recoveries or of episodes of inflation and disinflation.

Scanning across the remaining columns of Figure 10, we can see that every column in which the Treasury Bill rate shows substantial movement shows movement in the same direction by P and Pcm. The first monetary policy column is the only one in which interest rates and either price variable show any substantial movement in opposite directions. This suggests both that none of the other columns are heavily contaminated with monetary policy shock components, and that a large fraction of the variance of interest rates must be attributed to systematic policy responses to the threat of inflation, not to erratic fluctuations in monetary policy. Here again, for the reasons discussed in the earlier section on method, this type of conclusion is robust to variations in the identification scheme.

The identification scheme for a larger model that adds to the 13-variable model some variables related to the banking sector (an index of rates on M2 deposits (RM2), bank holdings of securities (Bs), bank loans (Bl), and the prime interest rate (Rl)), the Federal Reserve discount rate, and the Funds rate.

Here as with the previous model, we estimated initially with soft zero constraints as shown in the table, obtained reasonable point estimates, but then found numerical difficulties in producing error bands. As with the other model, we found that converting the soft zeros to hard zeros eliminated the numerical difficulties while leaving the nature of the results largely unchanged. The results displayed are therefore all for the hard zero version of the model.

We display the impulse responses in Figure 12. Because there are two interest rates in this model that are naturally thought of as set by the Federal Reserve-the Federal Funds rate and the Discount rate-the first two columns of the figure are should be interpreted as responses to policy disturbances.

They are similar to the first column of Figure 10 in the rows where the variables are comparable, but here the first column apparently represents a short-lived tightening of policy and the second a longer-lived one. Because the two policy disturbances are distinguished only by an arbitrary normalization, "policy shocks" could take the form of any linear combination of these two columns.

Figure shows the responses to the two columns of policy shocks on a larger scale, and with 68% error bands. The first column's responses are fairly sharply determined, though slightly less sharply than the responses in the 13-variable model. The second column's responses mostly leave zero response within the range of high probability, except for responses of interest rates. We see that the first column's disturbance generates an outflow of M1 deposits, offset initially by a decline in bank securities but then later by a decline in bank loans.

This seems to be a reasonable pattern for the banking system's response to a monetary contraction, reinforcing the plausibility of our identification. The fact that Rf and Rd move in different patterns in the two columns shows that the two variables have considerable independent variation. But there seems to be only one column's worth of substantial non-interest-rate effects here. A policy action that moved Rf and Rd in the same direction by about the same amount would have effects that approximately sum. These would be slightly stronger for the most part than what appears in column 1 of that figure, but not very different on the whole.

This column is the t8h in the figure, but the first in theP sector. Also as in the 13-variable model, here we find prices and interest rates moving in the same direction in response to nearly all disturbances. In this case, though, there is one disturbance in the I sector, in addition to the main policy disturbance, that moves interest rates up and prices down-the 17th column.

This disturbance seems to have negligible real effects, and it involves a sharp, temporary movement in long rates that seems incommensurate with the small associated movements in Rf and Rd. Nonetheless, from the form of responses to it, it appears possible that this disturbance could-be contaminated with a monetary-poliey-shock component.

These results are basically easy to defend, but let us add a note of caution here. We are not sure of the implications of our numerical difficulties in the less restricted models that we initially thought more plausible than these. It could be that when we resolve them we will see that there is much more statistical uncertainty in these results than what is presented here would suggest. Also, we experimented with a version of the 18-variable model that included the three-month Treasury Bill rate in addition to the Funds rate. This version of the model proved quite capable of producing the kind of identification confusion we discussed in the context of the example model of equations (4)-(5) above.

A reasonable-looking fitted model, after some small change in specification or sample period, might show "impulse response rotation", with what looked like a monetary policy shock emerging as an I sector shock, while the shock formally identified as a monetary policy shock ceased to make sense. This is exactly the pattern that would be expected if the Treasury Bill rate were tightly linked to the Funds rate by term-structure arbitrage relationships and contained little information useful to policy authorities. As we pointed out in our discussion above, in such circumstances including the Bill rate in the model can weaken identification without improving the accuracy of the model.

We think therefore that we are justified in reacting to these difficulties by looking at a model without the Treasury Bill rate, but it would of course be more satisfactory to find a way to model the two short rates jointly while maintaining robust identification.

CONCLUSION

What we have presented here is clearly far from the last word on these issues, even in the context of identified VAR research. It remains quite possible, for example, that we are still attributing to policy disturbances some variation that actually originates in adverse supply shocks. This would tend to attenuate the estimated price-reducing effects of monetary contraction and exaggerate the estimated output-reducing effects. With similar methods, using smaller models, Soyoung Kim [1995] finds very small real effects and larger price effects using data for other countries, and Cushman and Zha [1994], exploiting the identification possibilities that arise for a small open economy, also find small real effects.

Nonetheless we regard our estimates as having some chance of being about right. We think that using the larger modeling framework makes it possible to get a clearer understanding of what the identification problems are, and to become more confident in interpreting results as we trace effects across a wider variety of variables. We believe that we have rather firmly established the unreliability of identifications that treat a monetary aggregate, whether reserves or an M variable, as moving mainly in response to policy disturbances in the short run.

The bulk of movements in both aggregates arise from policy accommodating private sector demand shifts. And we believe we have confirmed that most movements in monetary policy instruments are responses to the state of the economy, not random deviations by the monetary authorities from their usual patterns of behavior. To policy analysts, accustomed to basing policy recommendations on current and expected economic conditions, this finding is surely unsurprising, but it should nonetheless be disturbing. It implies that careful attention to modeling of the policy-setting process is essential to accurate statistical assessment of the effects of policy. Much existing empirical policy modeling ignores or treats casually the implications of policy endogeneity. We hope to have demonstrated that careful treatment of policy endogeneity is feasible, as well as important.

DATA

All data are monthly from July 1959 to March 1996.

Rf = Federal funds rate, effective rate, percent per annum.

Rd = discount window borrowing rate at the Federal Reserve Bank of New York, percent per annum.

TR = total reserves, adjusted for breaks due to changes in reserve requirements, SA, Bil.$.

TRU = total reserves, not adjusted for breaks due to changes in reserve requirements, SA, Bil.$.

RM2 = M2 own rate of return: deposit-weighted averages of annual effective yields on deposits in M2.

BS = Securities at all commercial banks, SA, Bil.$: computed as total loans and securities at all commercial banks less total loans and leases at all commercial banks.

BL = Total loans and leases at all commercial banks, SA, Bil.$.

RL = Prime rate on short-term business loans, average of daily figures, percent per annum.

M1 = M1 money stock, SA, Bil.$.

M2* = M2 money stock less M1 money stock, SA, Bil.$.

Y = real gross domestic product, SA, Bil. Chain 1992$: monthly series interpolated from national income and product accounts quarterly series using Chow-Lin procedure with underlying monthly data on total industrial production, civilian employment 16 years or older, retail sales deflated by consumer prices, real personal consumption expenditures, and the National Association of Purchasing Managers' Composite Index.

INR = real private non-residential fixed investment, SA, Bil. Chain 1992$: monthly series interpolated from national income and product accounts quarterly private non-residential fixed investment series using Chow-Lin procedure with underlying monthly data on real value of new construction of privately owned nonresidential industrial structures, total equipment component of industrial production, industrial machinery and equipment component of industrial production, intermediate products and business supplies component of industrial production, manufacturers' shipments to capital goods industries, and manufacturers' shipments of construction materials, supplies, and intermediate products.

IR = real residential fixed investment, SA, Bil. Chain 1992$: monthly series interpolated from national income and product accounts quarterly private residential fixed investment series using Chow-Lin procedure with underlying monthly data on housing starts, construction supplies component of industrial production, manufacturers' shipments of construction materials, supplies, and intermediate products, and real value of new construction of privately owned residential buildings.

P = consumer price index for urban consumers, total, SA.

U = civilian unemployment rate, SA, percent.

R3 = 3-month Treasury bill rate, secondary market, percent per annum.

Pc = crude materials component of the producers' price index, SA.

Pcm = IMF index of world commodity prices.

R10 = 10-year Treasury bond yield, constant maturity, percent per annum.

E = trade-weighted value of the U.S. dollar, Atlanta Fed index, 1980=100.

The Prior

For sufficient detail on the prior to actually use our methods, and for an appreciation of the numerical and mathematical considerations that led us to this particular form, refer to Sims and Zha [1996]. Here we outline our approach. We postulate a joint normal prior, initially with diagonal covariance matrix, on the elements of A0 that are not constrained to zero. In the case of reduced form models, we choose an ordering of the variables in which to constrain A0 to be triangular, an exactly identified normalization. We then specify a joint normal prior on all the coefficients in As, s 0 conditional on A0.

To make the prior center on specifications in which reduced form models for individual variables are random walks, we make the conditional mean of A1 | A0 be A0 itself, while the conditional mean of As | A0, s 1 is zero. The prior standard deviations of the elements of the As matrices shrink with increasing s, and these elements are initially taken as uncorrelated. It may seem that this approach, constructing the prior from a marginal on A0 and a conditional distribution for As | A0, s 1, is roundabout and complicated, but it turns out to be critical to making the method numerically feasible in large models. On this base prior we then layer additional components, constructed as "dummy observations".

The dummy observations induce correlations across elements of A in the prior. The dummy observations express beliefs that no-change forecasts of the model's variables are likely to be quite good. Of special note is that in large dynamic systems like this, the same phenomenon that leads to the well-known bias toward stationarity of least squares estimators leads to a bias toward explaining implausibly large fractions of the historically observed variation in the data with deterministic components of the model.

We found that dummy observations of this "no-change-forecasts should be good" type also express the belief that models that explain too much with deterministic components are implausible. It appears that using such dummy observations is essential to getting sensible results in models of this scale, yet conventional time series diagnostic testing might not reveal situations where this bias is distorting results. This point is discussed further in Sims and Zha [1996].

Though these priors may seem complicated, they were not influential in determining the character of the results. In small models, where the bias toward excessively strong deterministic components is not great, results with a flat prior and with our prior look quite similar. The prior tends to make the estimated impulse responses smoother without changing their overall form. The prior was not manipulated to make results look more reasonable, except in the case of the "soft zero constraints" in the prior on A0 that were discussed in the text.

INFORMATION ON THE MEETING OF THE MONETARY POLICY COUNCIL ON SEPTEMBER 24-25, 2002

The Monetary Policy Council held its meeting on September 24-25, 2002. The Council was submitted the materials prepared by the Management Board and departments of the NBP as well as information and analytical materials prepared by the Ministry of Finance, banks and research institutes. The Council discussed the external conditions of the Polish economy and tendencies in the real sector of the economy, in the area of wages and social benefits, in public finance sector, in the area of money supply, lending and interest rates, and the formation of inflation expectations, prices and the inflation outlook.

DECISION OF THE MONETARY POLICY COUNCIL

In September, the enhancement of a low inflation level is observed. Factors that reduce inflation growth in future have strengthened:

- o the expected within 12 months level of inflation has been subject to further reduction,
- o the current inflation rate and all core inflation measures lowered,
- o the dynamics of money supply M3 dropped,
- o the dynamics of lending to households and businesses lowered significantly,
- o a moderate growth of wages-in conditions of a high level of unemployment-does not threaten in a form of the increased inflation pressure,
- o the growth forecasts for the world economy lowered, including, in particular, the German economy.

The signals coming from the economy are still not explicit. Positive information on the increase of the estimate value of newly begun investments can forecast a coming improvement of the investment demand. We assess that the data for August on the sold industrial output, although a little weaker than it was commonly expected, confirm that the lowering trend in production has been overcome and the increase of the added value in this sector should be expected in the 3rd quarter. These signals give the evidence that the economic growth pace will increase in the quarters to come.

Whether the slow economic growth accelerates considerably and whether this acceleration is permanent will be decided by the demand driven factors and mainly the demand from abroad. The growth forecasts for abroad, however, are not optimistic. The prudence in the assessment of possibilities of the investment demand dynamics acceleration is also prompted by the higher risk of a war with Iraq.

A moderate pace of the economic boom, according to the Council, does not pose a threat to the accomplishment of the inflation target in 2002 and 2003 at the moment, however, it indicates the necessity to be prudent in making decisions on the pace and scale of the monetary policy loosening.

Factors that could threaten the stabilization of inflation at a low level and limit the growth of production potential are still observed:

- o the drop of the annualized dynamics of household deposits is getting deeper,
- o there is still maintained significant uncertainty related to fuel prices,
- o the draft Act on the State Budget for the year 2003 does not constitute the fulfillment of the Government's earlier declarations to take measures that would permanently improve the situation in public finance. The draft lacks the basic systemic solutions that would affect the reduction of the budget expenses dynamics and change their structure. The outlook of maintaining a high deficit of the public finance sector in the conditions of a forecasted faster economic growth in 2003 means further loosening of fiscal policy.

The Monetary Policy Council acknowledged that, from the point of view of future inflation, factors reducing the inflation pressure have got-on the basis of present forecasts- a bigger impact than factors threatening the inflation stabilization and decided to:

- o cut the minimum yield on 28-day open market operations from 8.0% to 7.5%;
- o cut the rediscount rate from 9.0% to 8.5%;
- o cut the lombard rate from 10.5% to 10.0%;
- o cut the deposit rate from 5.5% to 5.0%;
- o maintain its neutral position in monetary policy.

The next meeting of the Monetary Policy Council will be held on October 3, 2002.

Evaluation of the Economic Situation

The economic growth in the 2nd quarter this year as compared to the same quarter of the previous year amounted to 0.8% and at the scale of the first six months 0.6%. The improvement of the economic growth in the 2nd quarter this year mainly resulted from thc increase of private consumption (2.9%) and a lower than in the previous quarters drop of gross investments in fixed assets (-8.4%).

The currently available statistical data, however, still do not give the reason for the explicitly positive evaluation of the present economic situation what prompts being prudent about the outlook for a fast growth of the dynamics of GDP in 2003.

On one hand, the data on a gradual increase of the activity in the real sector-the dynamics of the industrial production, retail sales, get confirmed. On the other hand, however, the evaluations of the external demand growth that is a basic factor affecting investment decisions worsened. A high level of unemployment reduces both the wage demands and the increase of consumption. Therefore, in the next couple of months, a faster growth of income from hired labor should not be expected. Together with a low growth of income from social benefits, it forecasts a further weakening of consumer demand growth.

The survey of the economic situation of enterprises from the processing industry sector, construction and trade made in August did not reflect firm symptoms of the economic boom. The evaluation of a general climate of the economic situation-considering seasonal fluctuations -is still negative, although a little better than a month before.

The next month did not bring the improvement of feelings of enterprises and households both in the USA and in the euro zone. In the American economy, the indices illustrating both the business climate of households and the activity in the manufacturing sector are getting lower. In Germany, the leading for the manufacturing sector index of the institute Ifo lowered from 91.6 in May to 88.8 in August this year.

The factor that is the most uncertain is the formation of oil prices worldwide. The increase of political risk resulted in the situation that in the 1st half of September 2002 an average oil price amounted to almost USD 28 per barrel, so it was higher by USD 1 than in August this year. It is estimated that at present the risk of the war affects the increase of oil prices by at least USD 5 per barrel.

Situation in Public Finance Sector

The situation of the state budget in 2002 as compared to the situation analyzed last month did not change. In August, the state budget accomplishment was according to the plan what gives the evidence that there is no threat of exceeding the defined level of budget deficit. There is a possibility, however, that the revenues from indirect taxes will be smaller in the 4th quarter this year than it would result from tendencies observed in previous months. It results from systemie changes that will become effective and the most important of which is enabling small businesses to file their value added taxes quarterly what will result in the shift of some of such due receivables to the year 2003.

Due to the above mentioned, at the end of this year there may be a necessity to reduce expenses in order to meet the defined deficit limit what, in practice, would mean carrying forward some of the reduced expenses for the year 2003 and thus a bigger burden for the budget next year.

The economic deficit of the public finance sector this year will probably be at the significantly higher level than 4.8% of GDP that is set forth in the Act on the State Budget, mainly as a result of big shortages of earmarked funds. The guidelines of the draft act on the state budget for the year 2003 presented by the Minister of Finance indicate that when cyclical factors are considered, the fiscal policy would be loosened.

This situation will not be supported by increased budget revenues through the assumption of too optimistic macroeconomic forecasts, as well as single measures bringing additional revenues such as tax abolition and restructuring fees.

The Government did not fulfill the principle of the real growth of central budget expenses by 1% as it declared, since the expenses are to increase in real terms by 2.2% and to amount to PLN 193.5 billion.

Money Supply, Loans, Interest Rates, Exchange Rate

The annualized dynamics of money supply M3 lowered, and at the same time, the dynamics of cash stabilized, but the dynamics of deposits drops what is the evidence of a weakening tendency to save at banks as a result of the drop of attractiveness of bank placements.

A low dynamics of lending to households is maintained; its annualized pace amounted to 8.5% in August this year. The data for August did not confirm the increased activity in financing the enterprises by banks as it was observed in the previous months. The annualized pace of lending to enterprises amounted to 1.8% as compared to 2.7% in July this year.

In August and the 1st half of September, the tendency to the depreciation of the zloty was halted. It was mainly related to the halted appreciation of the euro on the world market. Due to the above mentioned, in August this year, the indices of the effective exchange rates of the zloty: the nominal one and the real ones practically stabilized at the level noted in July this year.

Prices, Inflation Expectations

In August this year, as a result of a further drop of foodstuff prices, the annualized consumer price index lowered from 1.3% to 1.2%. All core inflation measures lowered as well, although not as much as last month. According to the expectations, in August this year as compared to July this year the sold industrial output prices rose.

The annualized dynamics of these prices will probably be higher than in case of consumer prices within the next couple of months, and the factors affecting this dynamics will be high oil prices and a delayed effect of the zloty depreciation within the recent months.

Inflation on a low level supports the enhancement of low inflation expectations. In September this year, inflation expectations by both individuals and bank analysts lowered, and the drop of inflation expectations is related to both the expected inflation rates in December 2002 and in the 12-month horizon.

The inflation rate expected by bank analysts at the end of this year amounted to 1.8% what means its drop by 0.5 percentage point as compared to the declarations made in August this year, and the expected annualized inflation rate (August 2003) amounted to 2.9% what means its drop by 0.2 percentage point.

4

CORPORATE DISCLOSURE AND CAPITAL MARKETS

INTRODUCTION

There is increasing pressure from the capital markets on companies to operate in an accountable and transparent manner, whether it is shareholder pressure on banks to disclose ethical risks or institutional investors demanding climate risk disclosure. Credible disclosure of all aspects of a company's performance-financial, economic, environmental, social and ethical-is becoming an increasingly important way to enhance corporate accountability and transparency and to inform the capital markets.

The National Round Table on the Environment and the Economy (NRTEE) is engaged in a multi-year program to explore the relationship between capital markets, financial performance and sustainability in Canada.

With the Capital Markets and Sustainability program, the NRTEE hopes to facilitate a multi-stakeholder debate on responsible investment and corporate responsibility (CR) by exploring the links between CR (comprising environmental and social issues) and financial performance in Canada.

SHAREHOLDER PERSPECTIVES

Canadian public survey research conducted in 2003 captured shareholder perspectives on issues related to the capital markets and corporate disclosure:

- 90% of Canadians support "requiring companies to publicly report their social and environmental performance."
- 84% of Canadian shareholders believe that the "financial community should pay more attention to social and environmental performance when valuing companies."
- More than 80% of Canadians support "requiring pension funds to publicly report whether or not they take the social and environmental performance of the companies they invest in into consideration."

This study is intended to support the NRTEE Capital Markets and Sustainability Program by providing a characterization of the current demand for and supply of CR information in Canada and elsewhere.

On the demand side, Section 2 provides a characterization of the capital markets (pension funds, investment management companies, etc.) and an overview of the types of CR information the various segments of the capital markets are starting to request. On the supply side, Section 3 describes the types of information selected companies in the oil and gas, mining, and financial services sectors are disclosing on some key issues: climate change for oil and gas, biodiversity for the mining sector, and environmental and social risk in lending and project financing for the financial services sector.

The section also briefly summarizes how companies in each of these sectors disclose information about regulatory compliance. Based on these findings, Section 4 provides preliminary recommendations for the capital markets and for reporting companies, as well as recommendations with respect to ways in which public policies could promote corporate disclosure to help capital markets value responsible corporate practices in Canada, and therefore encourage responsible investment.

> *"Full disclosure of material information by publicly owned companies is obviously crucial for the efficient functioning of capital markets and for the protection of investors..."*
>
> *Robert Repetto, Stratus Consulting*
>
> *"Better disclosure builds confidence."*
>
> *Deb Abbey, President, Real Assets Investment Management Inc.*

Methodology and Terminology

Methodology

The study presented in this report was based on the following methodology.

First, we reviewed publications that address the sustainability information demands of stakeholders in the capital markets (e.g., reports from the Carbon Disclosure Project and the United Nations Environment Programme Finance Initiative (UNEP FI), see References). We used this information to map the types of sustainability information the various segments of the capital markets are demanding.

Second, we interviewed a small number of stakeholders in the capital markets (e.g., investment analyst, credit risk analyst, rating agency analyst, pension fund manager) to determine the kinds of sustainability information capital markets value and that Canadian corporations should be reporting. Appendix 1 provides the questionnaire used.

Third, to understand how companies are disclosing information on specific issues, we reviewed the publicly available information produced by corporations in selected sectors.

This review covered a range of disclosure mechanisms, including sustainability reports, annual reports (including Management's Discussion and Analysis), audited financial statements, annual information forms, investor bulletins and corporate Web sites.

It is important to emphasize that this study is based on a review of published information by companies. The findings presented therefore reflect what companies are disclosing, and may not necessarily include references to all of the policies, management systems and activities the companies reviewed may actually be engaged in.

The study team selected the five Canadian companies in each sector that met the largest number of the following criteria:

(1) Companies were first screened using the listing of the 1000 largest publicly traded Canadian corporations, measured by assets, in The Globe and Mail's Report on Business.3

(2) These companies were then screened based on the availability of a current sustainability report or an annual report with at least five pages of environmental and/or social information, as well as specific performance data.

(3) The third screening criterion was the comparability of each company's operations with those of other companies within the sector. Comparable operations facilitate the identification of relevant material issues.

(4) The fourth screening criterion was recognition as a sustainability leader by inclusion on the Dow Jones

Sustainability Index, the Jantzi Social Index or the FTSE4 Good Index.

These criteria inevitably result in a focus on leading companies within each sector. The following table lists the companies included in the study.

OIL AND GAS	MINING	FINANCIAL SERVICES
Imperial Oil	Barrick Gold	Bank of Montreal
Nexen	Falconbridge-Noranda	Bank of Nova Scotia
Petro-Canada	Inco	Canadian Imperial Bank of Commerce
Shell Canada	Inmet Mining	Royal Bank of Canada
Suncor Energy	Teck Cominco	Toronto-Dominion Bank

To analyze the supply of sustainability information, we used a tool 4designed to facilitate a high-level assessment of how companies are disclosing information against key elements related to the effective management of the study issues, including the perform ..nce indicators used. The four key disclosure elements reviewed are policy and strategy; governance structures; management systems; and monitoring, reporting and assurance.

Terminology

There are various terms used to describe a company's performance in non-traditional financial areas. Social, environmental and ethical (SEE) issues are often referred to. Sustainability and corporate responsibility encompass broader economic performance (e.g., direct economic impact on communities), social performance (e.g., workplace relations or business ethics) and environmental performance. In this study, we use the terms sustainability, corporate responsibility and non-traditional financial information interchangeably when referring to a company's economic, environmental, social and ethical performance.

DEMAND FOR CORPORATE RESPONSIBILITY DISCLOSURE

Capital Markets Characterization

For the purpose of this study, the capital markets are divided into six segments, each of which provides distinct services such as credit and loans, risk underwriting, property and casualty insurance, and equity investment. 5Figure 1 provides a characterization of these different segments in Canada, including their market profile and assets under management.

Figure: Characterization of Canadian Capital Markets

Segment	Market Profile	Assets
Commercial Banks	Accept deposits and extend credit to serve consumer and corporate needs for capital.	The Canadian banking industry includes 19 domestic banks, 30 foreign bank subsidiaries and 23 foreign bank branches. In total, these institutions manage almost $1.8 trillion in assets (Canadian Bankers Association 2004).
Investment Banks	Generally focus on equity investments. Generate revenue by charging a fee for transactions, which include initial public offerings (IPOs), mergers and acquisitions, divestitures, liquidations, and private placements. Unlike commercial banks, tend to have little or no stake in long-term transactions.	$10.6 billion in revenues in 2003, 73 percent ($7.7 billion) of which is generated by the securities firms associated with the six largest domestic banks (Department of Finance 2005)
Investment Management Companies	Raise capital for investing in financial instruments, including stocks, bonds and money markets. Mutual fund unit holders pay a fee to have their money managed. Each mutual fund is established with a specific investment strategy and objectives. A small but growing number of investment management companies focus on socially responsible investment (SRI), applying screens to exclude or favour certain companies based on social, environmental and ethical criteria.	Mutual fund industry assets were $391 billion as of December 2002 (Department of Finance 2004). Total SRI assets managed in Canada reached $51.4 billion—3.3% of the retail mutual fund and institutional investment market—in the same time period (Social Investment Organisation 2003).

Pension Funds	A means for individuals to save for their retirement. In defined contribution plans the employee/employer puts aside a set amount each pay period. Defined benefit plans guarantee the employee a set benefit upon retirement. Tend to have a longer-term investment horizon because of relatively stable inflows (contributions) and outflows (benefits).	Approximately $600 billion in assets under management (Statistics Canada 2002).
Insurance and Re-insurance Companies	a) Property and Casualty Insurance: Underwrites risk, investment management. Composed of three categories: – primary insurers, re-insurers and "excess" insurers. Re-insurers and "excess" insurers take a more global approach, both in geographic markets and products, to spread risk. b) Life Insurance: Sell life insurance policies to consumers and invest the funds from the premiums of these policies. Generate revenue by charging premiums calculated to exceed claims and from capital and interest from its investments. One of the largest pools of investment capital in the world.	a) Property and Casualty Insurance: Control assets of more than $80 billion (Insurance Bureau of Canada 2004). b) Life Insurance: At the end of 2002, Canada's life and health insurers held $279.5 billion in assets on behalf of policyholders. Most was invested in Canada's economy, primarily in government bonds ($63.5 billion), corporate bonds ($56.5 billion), stocks ($37.2 billion), mutual funds ($41.5 billion), commercial mortgage loans ($22.5 billion) and residential mortgage loans ($17.5 billion).
Index Providers	Provide an index tool for investors and asset managers to identify and invest in companies that meet a CR or sustainability benchmark. Criteria often differentiated by sector.	

Characterization of Information Demands

There is a growing understanding among the different actors within these segments of the capital markets-lenders, fund managers, institutional investors-that CR performance and management can affect shareholder value both positively and negatively. A 2003 report involving nine of the largest stock brokerage firms in the world concluded that environmental, social and corporate governance criteria are relevant to long-term shareholder value. Similarly, 79 percent of the European fund managers and financial analysts surveyed in a 2003 study stated that the management of social and environmental risks has a positive impact on a company's market value over the long-term.

"The Canada Pension Plan Investment Board believes that responsible corporate behaviour-in such matters as the environment, employee practices, stakeholder relations, human rights, respect for domestic and international laws, and ethical conduct-generally contributes to enhanced long-term investment returns. Therefore, investment analysis, due diligence and monitoring of Canadian and foreign investments should take corporate behaviour into account."

Canada Pension Plan Social Investment Policy

The demand for improved CR information and for more systematic use of that information by the capital markets is coming from seven main sources:

- Socially responsible investment or responsible investment (RI) funds are responsible for much of the increased salience of CR information. Nearly 50 percent of Europe's financial institutions now offer RI products (CSR Europe et al. 2003). In Canada, RI funds have grown; total RI assets managed in Canada in 2003 were $51.4 billion or 3.3 percent of the retail mutual fund and institutional investment market (Social Investment Organisation 2003). Most projections suggest that although it is fast-growing, RI will remain a relatively small segment of the overall investment community.
- Financial indices that incorporate environmental and social criteria are increasing in number. Examples include the Dow Jones Sustainability Indexes, the FTSE4Good and the Canadian-based Jantzi Social Index. The profile of these indices is also increasing, as companies want to be listed to gain recognition

as sustainable performers. Some companies are responding to this development by improving their CR performance reporting. Others are including social responsibility as a topic in investor briefings.

- Shareholders have been filing resolutions in escalating numbers, as well as increasingly supporting resolutions that demand disclosure of social and/or environmental performance information from companies. In Canada, this increase in shareholder activism is attributed in part to amendments to the Canadian Business Corporations Act, which allow shareholders to communicate more freely about the development of resolutions, provide greater scope for minority shareholder resolutions, and narrow the rules permitting companies to exclude resolutions. Certain sectors have been targeted by shareholder action. The oil and gas sector, for example, has been targeted on climate change disclosure and renewable energy strategies, and at least seven Canadian banks have faced resolutions demanding disclosure on social, ethical and environmental risks.

- Financial institutions are using their combined influence (i.e., enormous sums of investment funds) to create pressure for improved performance and enhanced disclosure on specific issues. Under the Carbon Disclosure Project, for example, institutional investors representing $10 trillion in assets are demanding disclosure of the financial risk of carbon emissions from the Fortune 500 companies. Participating investment firms in Canada include the Ontario Teachers Pension Plan Board, Acuity Investment Management Inc. and CI Mutual Funds. Similarly, thirteen major public pensions in the United States, representing more than US$800 billion, recently asked the US Securities and Exchange Commission to require corporate disclosure of global warming risks. Similar initiatives focus on specific practices in specific sectors (child labour in the garment industry, for example).

- Oversight bodies and regulators in both Europe and North America have initiated measures to enhance the impact of existing disclosure requirements. In 2001, the US Environmental Protection Agency (EPA) began efforts to share more environmental performance data with securities regulators in an effort to raise awareness of the "materiality" of this information (US EPA 2001). In 2001, the European Commission issued stricter but non-binding guidelines for the disclosure of environmental costs and liabilities. And in November 2002, the Canadian Institute of Chartered Accountants (CICA) published a voluntary guidance document emphasizing the importance of including all material risks as well as environmental and social performance drivers in the Management's Discussion and Analysis, which is usually included in the annual report. A new area being addressed by the CICA and the bodies that set international accounting standards is how to account for and report on transactions related to greenhouse gas reductions, emission allowances, and other climate change exposures-whether market-based or regulatory (CICA 2004).
- New regulatory obligations related to disclosure are being introduced by a growing number of jurisdictions. The Sarbanes-Oxley Act requires Chief Executive Officers in the United States to sign-off on the accuracy of the statements they make in corporate and annual reports, including those related to the environmental and social aspects of business practice.

As of September 1, 2004, a new rule from the US Securities and Exchange Commission (SEC) came into force requiring mutual funds to disclose their proxy voting records to shareholders online or in paper form, as requested (US SEC 2004). The SEC will also make the information available on its Web site. The Canadian Securities Administrators have proposed a similar rule, which would require investment funds to establish policies and procedures for voting proxies and to maintain a proxy voting record available to unit holders on request. This rule was disseminated for consultation in the summer of 2004, and could come into force early in 2005. Various European countries have also added new requirements to disclose environmental, social and ethical considerations (e.g., pension fund legislation in the United Kingdom, French security legislation). Most recently, the Italian government passed legislation requiring pension funds to disclose the non-financial considerations they take into account when making investment decisions. In Canada, the Public Statements of Accountability Regulations require additional social and economic disclosure from some financial institutions.

- Finally, a wide variety of awareness-raising initiatives have been developed, from the UNEP FI to various civil society initiatives to the ongoing NRTEE initiative.

Each of these sources has influenced the increasing disclosure and consideration of non-traditional financial information. An analysis of the demand by capital markets for such disclosure and the supply of financially relevant CR information by corporations is presented in the following sections.

Analysis of Information Demands from Capital Markets

"Many Canadians believe that there is more to share ownership than supporting profit-making to improve short-term share price. We agree ... In addition, we believe that disclosure is the cornerstone that allows investors to better understand long-term risks. Consequently, we support reasonable shareholder resolutions that ask companies to make full disclosure on issues that relate to social responsibility, ethical behaviour, sustainable development and corporate citizenship."

CANADA PENSION PLAN INVESTMENT BOARD

This section analyzes, by example, the types of CR information being sought by the different capital market segments as part of the financial analyses they make in their business decision-making. Appendix 3 provides a more detailed mapping of these demands.

Commercial Banks

In Canada, commercial banks are demanding a relatively limited scope of corporate responsibility information. These information demands primarily relate to credit and lending risk assessment and decision-making, including lender liability. In terms of CR considerations used by leading banks, environmental risks appear to bc morc systematically assessed than are social risks, which are more qualitatively assessed.

Demands focus mainly on environmental risks related to property contamination and compliance issues. A company's exposure to environmental, legal and major event risks (e.g., impending regulation) is a consideration in most commercial bank credit and lending decisions. Most banks are viewing climate change as an increasingly important issue in the oil and gas sector, but there is a view that a regulatory framework needs to be in place to assess this comprehensively.

Some commercial banks in Canada are signatories to the Equator Principles, which incorporate environmental and social considerations into large project financing decisions.

The Equator Principles include social considerations such as the human rights risks in a country where the proponent project is to be located. One large Canadian bank applies the Equator Principles to project financing as an internal policy requirement, using a threshold below the $50 million project size specified in the principles.

Statement of Principles

Note: this is a general summary of the principles and excludes some details.

1. We have categorised the risk of a project in accordance with internal guidelines based upon the environmental and social screening criteria.
2. The borrower has completed an Environmental Assessment (EA).
3. In the context of the business of the project, as applicable, the EA report has addressed:
   a) assessment of the baseline environmental and social conditions
   b) requirements under host country laws and regulations, applicable international treaties and agreements
   c) sustainable development and use of renewable natural resources

d) protection of human health, cultural properties, and biodiversity, including endangered species and sensitive ecosystems

e) use of dangerous substances

f) major hazards

g) occupational health and safety

h) fire prevention and life safety

i) socioeconomic impacts

j) land acquisition and land use

k) involuntary resettlement

l) impacts on indigenous peoples and communities

m) cumulative impacts of existing projects, the proposed project, and anticipated future projects

n) participation of affected parties in the design, review and implementation of the project

o) consideration of feasible environmentally and socially preferable alternatives

p) efficient production, delivery and use of energy

q) pollution prevention and waste minimization, pollution controls (liquid effluents and air emissions) and solid and chemical waste management

Note: In each case, the EA will have addressed compliance with applicable host country laws, regulations and permits required by the project.

4. The borrower or third party expert has prepared an Environmental Management Plan (EMP), which draws on the conclusions of the EA.

5. We are satisfied that the borrower or third party expert has consulted, in a structured and culturally

appropriate way, with project affected groups, including indigenous peoples and local NGOs.

6. The borrower has covenanted to:
   a) comply with the EMP in the construction and operation of the project
   b) provide regular reports, prepared by in-house staff or third party experts, on compliance with the EMP, and
   c) where applicable, decommission the facilities in accordance with an agreed Decommissioning Plan.
7. As necessary, lenders have appointed an independent environmental expert to provide additional monitoring and reporting services.
8. In circumstances where a borrower is not in compliance with its environmental and social covenants, such that any debt financing would be in default, we will engage the borrower in its efforts to seek solutions to bring it back into compliance with its covenants.
9. These principles apply to projects with a total capital cost of $50 million or more.

Investment Banks

Similar to commercial banks, investment banks in Canada take a risk management approach and therefore focus on compliance issues and major crises. There is little documentation of the specific information demands of this segment of the capital markets. In an interview, an investment bank analyst for the mining sector explained that investment banks emphasize information related to risks associated with an investment prospect's environmental and social performance.

The key consideration appears to be whether the investment prospect is well placed to manage social and environmental risks (e.g., environmental regulatory approvals, labour disputes, forced resettlement, reclamation). If not, the investment bank may either decide to give a higher discount rate to lending or extend the time-frame analysis needed to complete the project, which affects the rate of return and the lending decision itself.

Thus, for this institution, environmental and social issues for project financing are considered in so far as they have a direct bearing on the financial analysis of the project (for example, the effect of the likely timing of project approval on the project rate of return).

Environmental and social risks are considered in relation to both the project proponent seeking financing (e.g., the strength of its environmental policies and management systems, its compliance record or its reputation for community relations) and to the host country/region (e.g., whether there is a record of timely or slow permitting processes, human rights considerations).

Investment banks will discount the financial return and, therefore, their lending decisions based on these factors. But they will not "pay a premium" for good environmental or social performance. However, they refuse to lend to, or take an equity interest in, projects in countries they deem to be politically unstable or too risky in terms of human rights and security concerns.

Investment Management Companies

There is some indication that mainstream investment management companies are beginning to make environmental and social information demands on companies, in order to develop new specialty investment products. Goldman Sachs, for example, has created an

Energy Environmental and Social Index, in which it accounts for issues such as climate change, pollution, human rights, management of diversity, safety and transparency.

In the United Kingdom, Morley Fund Management has taken a more integrated approach to environmental and social issues in its investment process. Morley has stated that it expects all of the Financial Times Stock Exchange (FTSE) 100 companies to publish a comprehensive environmental report or it will vote against the resolution to adopt the company's annual report and accounts at the annual general meeting.

Investment management companies in Canada have not been as active in demanding CR information from the companies in which they invest. There are a small number of companies that are either focused entirely on SRI or that have developed specific SRI products. Acuity Investment Management, for example, is involved in the UNEP FI Asset Management Working Group.

Responsible investment funds are also considered under this segment of the capital markets. As discussed earlier, information demands from this group are increasing and can be very specific in nature. For example, ISIS Asset Management in the United Kingdom seeks specific information related to biodiversity from the extractive industries in which it invests.

Pension Funds

In Canada, pension funds are currently focussed on issues of corporate risk, and particularly corporate governance. However, there is a growing indication that environmental and social considerations are being included in some pension fund investment analyses.

In Canada, the Canada Pension Plan Investment Board (CPPIB) is an important capital market player because of its large and growing market influence. Currently, CCPIB owns, on average, between two and three percent of more than 300 of Canada's largest public companies. Within the next decade, ownership is expected to increase to six or seven percent, positioning the CPPIB as a very influential shareholder of companies with widely dispersed shareholders.

The CPPIB has a detailed Social Investment Policy that addresses issues such as the environment, employee practices, stakeholder relations, human rights, respect for domestic and international laws, and ethical conduct. Similarly, the Statement of Investment Policies and Procedures for the Ontario Municipal Employees Retirement System (OMERS) "supports the notion that companies should publish and update in their annual reports their policies and procedures with respect to social, ethical and environmental issues that materially affect performance." Specific issues referenced include respect for employees, the environment, communities and human rights.

Pension funds use engagement with their investment target as the primary method to interact with companies they invest in, rather than submitting shareholder resolutions (Hebb 2004). Increasingly, however, pension funds are supporting resolutions submitted by other parties on disclosure of environmental and social performance information, and various pension plans have revised their proxy voting guidelines to allow them to do so.

A key objective of pension funds is to maximize their rate of return with the least risk so as to meet their primary objective of being able to fund the pension obligations as they come due. Within this context, a growing number of pension funds are recognizing and stating their understanding that a company's management of environmental and/or social issues can have a positive or negative impact on the long-term rate of return. Using financial statements as the main source of information, pension plan investors assess investment opportunities based on factors that may affect the likely long-term rate of return.

Although social and environmental factors tend not to dominate such analyses, their salience varies from sector-to-sector (e.g., they are more likely to be considered in mining than in retail). One pension fund analyst indicated that the large pension fund that he advises systematically assesses the potential of social and environmental risks to affect the long-term rate of return for companies operating in high-impact resource sectors such as mining and oil and gas.

This pension fund analyst seeks information on how the company manages CR risks (including climate change, human rights, waste management and community relations); has discussions with outside interests, including non-governmental organizations and host governments, to determine their CR-related concerns; and then makes a balanced assessment of whether the social or environmental risks are currently, or in the future, manageable in terms of their impact on financial return and share price. This same fund has flagged the "ethical behaviour" of companies in the financial services sector as a rapidly emerging risk area for investors.

As is discussed in the following section, recent work commissioned by the NRTEE concluded that current interpretations of the fiduciary duties of pension fund managers may unnecessarily constrain their ability to address the full range of relevant corporate responsibility considerations related to prospective investments. This is likely one reason why CR reviews not yet been mainstreamed in pension fund risk assessments.

Insurance and Re-Insurance Companies

The Canadian insurance industry as a whole has been less active in seeking CR-related information from its clients than have some of its foreign counterparts and some other institutional investors.

In the United Kingdom, the largest body representing insurers-the Association of British Insurers (ABI)-released disclosure guidelines that encourage companies to disclose information relating to their Boards' responsibilities for social, environmental and ethical (SEE) matters, as well as to specific policies, procedures and verification of SEE matters (no specific sub-issues are identified).

Internationally, the re-insurance sector-which is responsible for, among other things, covering losses associated with natural disasters-has become most interested in the climate change risk. Swiss Re, for example, has indicated that companies could find themselves losing protection against climate change-related liability claims for senior executives should they fail to adequately adopt climate change policies. Swiss Re is including questions on firms' climate change policies in the renewal notices that it sends out for directors' and officers' liability insurance.

Index Providers

Index providers rate companies on their performance, and companies want to be included in a range of indices to ensure that they have access to the widest number of potential shareholders. Responsible investment (RI) indices ask for very specific information and will also often indicate "the more the better" when it comes to corporate responsibility disclosure.

This is because the more information a company discloses, the more information RI index providers have available for assessing the company's management of the environmental and social factors they deem important (in the form of rating criteria).

The feeling is that the less they have to ask companies for additional information, the less likely it is that "survey fatigue" will occur. Many RI index providers support the idea of all companies producing standardized sustainability reports based on the Sustainability Reporting Guidelines developed by the Global Reporting Initiative (GRI).

Many of the RI indices examined as part of this study request specific information on a range of issues, including sustainability governance, stakeholder engagement, environmental management systems, greenhouse gas emissions and other air emissions, biodiversity, investment in intellectual capital, community investment, human resource management, diversity, human rights, compliance, and the independent verification of information.

RI index providers are the only capital market segment found by this survey to be asking companies to disclose performance and management information for specific environmental and social indicators.

Convergence of Demands

While it is hard to generalize about the precise type of disclosure demands being made by the Canadian capital markets as a whole, some trends are emerging.

- It is clear that demands are evolving rapidly, and that there is an increasing interest in general in CR information.
- Most segments of the capital markets pay at least some attention to the specific environmental or, in fewer cases, social issues faced by a company or project and how prepared the company is to manage these issues-but only if these issues are linked to

financial returns (project rate of return, or share value or shareholder earnings).

- Environmental or social issues are important only in terms of risk to the company's financial health, and therefore to capital market financial decision-making. High risk is discounted, but business opportunity from good sustainability performance is not given a premium in mainstream decision-making.
- Leading capital market players (i.e., those that are most progressive in terms of CR) in all segments have systematic processes for analyzing at least qualitatively-and in some cases quantitatively-the environmental management and performance information of companies they invest in or lend to. In some cases, processes are also in place for analyzing social management and performance, in qualitative terms, and incorporating it into financial decision-making. However, the depth of this capacity in each segment of the capital markets is limited and interest in these issues varies significantly even among organizations in similar capital market segments and lines of business.

In summary, there appears to be a fairly widespread, but only general, understanding of the negative implications of poor CR management. As a result, the predominant focus of the capital markets is on the ability of the organizations in which they are considering investing to manage environmental and, to a lesser degree, social risks. With relatively few exceptions, the capital markets do not account for the potential opportunities that may be associated with pro-active management of and performance on CR issues.

The significance of capital market demands for CR disclosure in most cases appears to be only modest. A survey of Chief Executive Officers carried out in 2002 by the World

Economic Forum asked business leaders to identify the stakeholder groups that created the greatest pressure or incentives for their CR activities. Investors ranked only seventh, indicating that they were not viewed as a primary driver (World Economic Forum and The Prince of Wales International Business Leaders Forum 2004, p. 5).

Some of the main impediments to the more systematic use of CR information by the capital markets include:

- prevailing interpretations of fiduciary duty;
- the dominant focus on short-term opportunities, with the exception of pension funds and RI indices;
- a widespread lack of awareness and understanding of the potential positive and negative links between CR management and corporate success over time; and
- the lack of standardized indicators, which impedes efforts to assess and compare performance among companies.

Nonetheless, key, financially relevant CR issues-which may vary by economic sector-appear to be emerging. Section 4 discusses four such issues: climate change for the oil and gas sector, biodiversity for the mining sector, environmental and social risk related to lending and project financing in the financial services sector, and compliance across all sectors.

Challenges Related to Information Demands

Despite the growing awareness of and demand for CR information on the part of certain members of the capital markets, overall demand by investors and others for CR information remains limited. In many cases, it appears that fund managers, analysts, investors and lenders rely on this information primarily in a negative sense. Poor social and environmental practices are seen as triggers for suspicion, whereas less than half of the respondents in a survey of European fund managers and financial analysts reported systematically seeking out evidence of good CR management or attributing a premium to companies with good CR performance (CSR Europe et al. 2003).

"The market does not pay a premium for good sustainability or environmental performance, but delivers a penalty if you do not [demonstrate competence in this regard]."12 In short, for many capital market actors, engagement in CR issues is seen as a proxy for good management, but does not stand on its own alongside financial results.

There are various reasons for the apparent lag in the demand for CR information relative to the understanding of its potential relevance to financial performance. Among the most important is the prevailing emphasis within the capital markets on short-term considerations such as quarterly results, and the strong belief that CR management is primarily relevant to the long-term value of a company.

However, most financial analysts appear to believe that CR management, if it is relevant, is only relevant in the short-term and from a negative perspective: whereas almost 80 percent of the fund managers and analysts surveyed in the 2003 CSR Europe study indicated that CR management has no positive impact in the short-term, 59 percent indicated that an environmental or social crisis can have an adverse short-term impact, primarily in terms of reputation.

The same survey reported that sell-side analysts are more sceptical about the impact of non-financial risks on share values than are fund managers and analysts (43 percent of sell-side analysts and 55 percent of fund managers and analysts believe non-financial risks affect share values) (CSR Europe et al. 2003).

Legal requirements also appear to play an important role in limiting the scope of consideration the various elements of the capital markets give to CR management. In 2003, the UNEP FI assembled the asset management working group (AMWG), a coalition of 12 asset managers from around the world. The AMWG undertook to explore and document the materiality of environmental, social and corporate governance considerations and criteria as they relate to the portfolio management of mutual and other institutional funds.

The AMWG's report concluded that capital markets should pay greater attention to sustainability management and performance, but that, among other things, the current definitions of the terms "fiduciary duty" and "financial materiality" may inhibit demand for and use of sustainability information. The AMWG report therefore recommended that governments and oversight bodies redefine these terms "to incorporate consideration of environmental, social and corporate governance criteria" (UNEP FI 2004, p. 5).

Other studies have come to similar conclusions. A study on environmental disclosure conducted by the US General Accounting Office (GAO) surveyed investor organizations, financial analysts and other experts who use disclosure information.

More than 75 percent of the respondents agreed that the guidance on assessing the likelihood of an environmental liability, determining when it must be disclosed and estimating its value is probably or definitely inadequate and therefore either probably or likely contributes to inadequate disclosure (US GAO 2004, pp. 53-54).

As is noted above, recent work on pension funds commissioned by the NRTEE produced similar findings. A related meeting of pension fund trustees and other practitioners convened by the NRTEE's Capital Markets and Sustainability Program concluded that there is a need to clarify, in regulation, that the consideration of SEE issues is not in conflict with the fiduciary duties of pension fund managers and trustees (NRTEE 2004, p. 1). In the same meeting, one participant in particular argued that new standards imposed by the accounting and actuarial professions and reinforced by regulators are unintentionally driving pension fund investment strategies to increasingly focus on the short term.

Poorly developed analytical techniques and limited awareness of the potential links between CR and corporate value also hinder the use of and demand for CR information. Even the most enthusiastic proponents of increasing the importance of CR considerations in capital markets acknowledge that demonstrating and quantifying the links between CR and corporate value is challenging.

A recent Conference Board of Canada (CboC) report observes that this is because CR performance correlates with a multitude of corporate activities that can affect share price, and because of the lack of a common analytical framework (CBoC 2003, p. 10). Assessing the links between CR and corporate value requires information about relevant issues, current performance and management capacity-each of which requires expertise and specialized analytical tools.

Moreover, the risks and benefits associated with CR issues and management are not uniform across all companies or sectors (ABI 2004), making it difficult to understand which companies are most affected by sustainability issues and which are most effective at managing those issues. Fortunately, some financial institutions are hiring or developing in-house expertise in the specific environmental and/or social "questions" to ask of companies in specific sectors.

The corollary of low demand is the fact that most companies are just learning how to communicate all relevant CR issues and practices in a way that is meaningful for the capital markets. Numerous studies in the past five years have documented widespread under-reporting of "material" environmental risks in financial reports in a wide range of sectors (Repetto 2004; Repetto and Henderson 2003; Austin and Sauer 2003; United States SEC 2003; Kiernan 2003; ABI 2004). Similarly, the growing profile of the GRI guidelines and the many initiatives to encourage greater and more standardized reporting of various sustainability issues suggests nascent but growing interest in learning how to communicate a set of issues that is only recently being recognized as material.

"Information is material if it would be considered important by an investor, acting reasonably, in making a decision to invest or continue to invest in the company. Management's determination of materiality applies not only to financial results but also to all information, qualitative as well as quantitative..."

CANADIAN INSTITUTE OF CHARTERED ACCOUNTANTS

The British organization AccountAbility and others have initiated various efforts to try to redefine the scope of material information that should be included in a sustainability report. AccountAbility recommends reporting on: short-term, direct financial impacts; performance against the company's own policies; business peer based norms; societal norms (regulations and emerging issues); and stakeholder concerns on issues that are reasonably likely to influence stakeholder behaviour (Zadek & Merme, 2003).

As discussed, investors are moving beyond short-term financial and technical risk for the basic reason that a wide range of issues can affect long-term financial performance. Environmental liabilities such as the decommissioning costs associated with an aging mine site-or liabilities associated with harmful products may and do have a direct impact on the value of a company, as may a wide range of other issues, such as the potential costs of non-compliance with existing environmental and social requirements; the possible implications of emerging requirements; and social or political risks such as human rights questions or community unrest in countries where a company operates.

Without adequate information, investment markets cannot operate efficiently, and there is growing evidence that the financial community is not adequately accounting for these issues. A review of the implications of climate change for institutional investors concluded, for example, that "climate risks are, in all probability, not being captured by existing financial analysis and so can provide additional information not currently captured in a firm's valuation" (Mansley and Dlugolecki 2001, p. 40). Similarly, studies show that companies facing significantly different environmental risks may have similar share prices because the market is unaware of the risk differentials (Repetto and Austin 2002). Recognizing these shortcomings, slightly over half of the European fund managers and financial analysts surveyed in the 2003 CSR Europe study predicted that social and environmental considerations would become a significant aspect of mainstream investment decision-making in the next two years. In Canada, and North America more broadly, there is no good picture or understanding of such latent demand.

5

CAPITAL MARKETS MANAGEMENT

INTRODUCTION

"It stands to reason that the best-managed companies deliver the best performance with regard to social and environmental issues and their interaction with the general business community. It is not surprising that they manage these issues as well as they manage the other more traditional success factors."

This is a widely held view of how the CR performance of companies is linked to financial performance.

"We strongly believe in full and consistent disclosure of CSR [Corporate Social Responsibility] data by companies so that they can be included in fundamental company analysis, where we believe that they belong. We see such issues as being an integral part of successful management in the modern world and that they should be taken into account in financial analysis and therefore investment considerations."

Anthony Ling, Co-Director of Research, Europe, Goldman Sachs

This view represents the emerging recognition that "quality of management" is not sufficient to assure financial success in the future. Financially relevant CR information will need to become an integral part of financial analysis as both internal business needs and external business conditions and societal expectations come to bear on a company's success.

To gain a better understanding of how companies are responding to these demands, we reviewed publicly available information provided by selected companies in three sectors. We looked at disclosure practices in relation to specific issues: climate change for the oil and gas sector, biodiversity for the mining sector, and environmental and social risk in lending and project financing for the financial services sector.

Disclosure of regulatory compliance was assessed across all sectors. These are considered "representative" CR issues for the purposes of the study and are not intended to indicate that other CR risks do not bear on capital-markets decision-making for these sectors.

For each issues, we focused on four elements:

- policy and strategy;
- governance structures;
- management systems; and
- performance, assurance and reporting.

This section discusses:

- trends in disclosure on the specific issues;
- best practices;
- what demands are being met and how;
- what demands are not being met; and
- characterization of challenges for why demands are not being met.

Oil and Gas Sector Disclosure of Climate Change Information

"The increased focus on climate change and corporate governance, together with the rise of socially responsible investment-managed money and non-governmental organisation activity, is taking place at a time when the energy industry is undergoing profound structural changes: the globalisation of the gas industry, the ability to invest on a truly global basis, and the creation of a more competitive and complicated industry with the rise of a new world order of emerging market players. This could be seen as either a threat or an opportunity, and we believe the responses of the companies to these issues will have a growing impact on performance and valuation."

Climate change issues are of obvious significance for the oil and gas sector for two main reasons. First, as a highly energy-intensive industry, the sector faces growing financial and regulatory pressure to reduce the greenhouse gas (GHG) emissions associated with its production activities. Companies in the sector are responding to this pressure through a combination of measures to enhance energy efficiency, utilize lower emitting or renewable forms of energy, and invest in carbon sequestration and offset projects. A second, but not so immediate, concern is the possibility that significant public policy interventions will stimulate a transition away from carbon-based fuels. This likely poses an even greater risk to long-term shareholder value.

Reflecting the salience of this issue for the sector, the five large oil and gas companies reviewed for this study all publicly disclose a considerable amount of information related both to their positions regarding climate change and to the steps they are taking to reduce their emissions. Overall, however, they each provide considerably more detail about their internal GHG reduction and offsetting activities and performance than about strategic plans to assess investments or other actions taken to address the potential long-term implications of a carbon-constrained future. The companies reviewed were Imperial Oil, Nexen, Petro-Canada, Shell Canada and Suncor.

Policy and strategy-Although none of the five companies reviewed has a formal policy on climate change, each has some form of environmental policy that includes commitments to prevent pollution or minimize emissions generically, and each describes the company's position regarding climate change. All five companies describe ongoing commitments to reduce GHG emissions from their own operations.

All five also state that they are involved in initiatives to help shape future public policy regarding climate change, although none provide specifics as to the precise policy positions they are advocating. Four of the five companies (Imperial Oil being the exception) state that they recognize that addressing climate change may require a long-term shift in the global energy mix. And three of the five describe ongoing commitments to seek out investment opportunities in non-carbon-based energy markets.

Imperial Oil is the major exception to this approach. It has posted several publications on its Web site regarding its position on climate change and its views on future energy demands. Its position on climate change is that the demand for energy will continue to grow, and will continue to be met largely by fossil fuels for the foreseeable future.

It states that addressing climate change will require a concerted, long-term effort to develop technologies that are more energy efficient or that use alternative fuels. As a result, Imperial Oil has very little public documentation regarding efforts to diversify its role as a supplier of carbon-based fuels. Rather, it states that its efforts are focused on reducing its own emissions and in investing (primarily through its parent company ExxonMobil) in technological research and development regarding cleaner energy and more efficient processes.

Although not specifically disclosed by the selected companies, companies that are members of the Canadian Association of Petroleum Producers (CAPP) are required to collect and report data related to GHG emissions as part of CAPP's Stewardship Initiative.

Governance-All of the companies disclose information on well-defined structures and processes for managing environmental impacts, including GHG emissions. Four of the five describe ongoing efforts to integrate climate change considerations into key decision-making points and processes, including business planning, risk evaluation and investment decision-making. Three of the companies also describe Board-level governance mechanisms specifically focused on climate change.

> *"In a rapidly globalizing, knowledge-based economy, sources of value creation in business are shifting from tangible assets such as land and equipment, to intangibles such as intellectual, human and social capital. While the relative importance of various assets is open to debate, we believe that relationships between a firm, its employees and other stakeholders constitute an important and yet undervalued business asset."*

Stakeholder engagement is a key aspect of sustainability management. Corporate disclosure of stakeholder engagement tends to focus on local issues; each of the companies we reviewed discloses information on local engagement processes with respect to ongoing environmental management issues. With respect to climate change activities (in terms of both reduced emissions and diversification strategies), however, the role that stakeholder engagement can play is very different. Most of the companies reviewed describe their involvement in the ongoing development of public policies around climate change.

Some describe their involvement in collaborative processes involving other businesses or NGOs to get "ahead" of policies. Shell Canada has an expert advisory panel focussed specifically on climate change. This represents a strategic management effort to understand the impact of climate change.

Management systems-By stating their belief that global efforts to address climate change may entail a long-term shift in the global energy mix, four of the five companies reviewed acknowledge that climate change represents a major business risk to be managed.

Three of the companies reviewed also describe processes they have in place to quantify and account for these risks with respect to ongoing and new investments. Suncor provides an estimate of the impact of Kyoto compliance on its ongoing operations. The business press reported this estimate widely when Suncor first made it public earlier this year. Nexen also discloses the potential cost of Kyoto compliance on its Long Lake Oil Sands Project.

All five companies describe mechanisms in place or being developed to integrate the management of GHG-reduction activities into ongoing operational management and assurance practices.

All five also describe programs to enhance employee awareness and to train employees in techniques and opportunities to enhance energy efficiency and reduce GHG emissions from operations.

Performance monitoring, reporting and assurance-All five of the companies provide reports of GHG emissions and plans to the Voluntary Challenge Reporting Registry. Each is also an active participant in the various ongoing activities within the sector to develop standardized units of-measure for energy intensity and GHG emissions. As a result, there is general comparability around reporting on absolute and normalized GHG emissions among the companies. Each of the five companies reports absolute GHG emissions (in kilotonnes of CO_2 equivalent).

Four of the five also report normalized emissions either in terms of tonnes of CO_2 equivalent per barrel of oil equivalent of production or per cubic meter produced. Four of the five use the Salomon Energy Intensity Index for reporting the energy intensity of downstream operations. Similarly, four of five use the CAPP Production Energy Intensity indicator for upstream operations.

Each also reports a quantitative target for energy efficiency and either a quantitative or qualitative target for GHG emission reductions. Finally, three of the five (Suncor, Petro-Canada and Shell) compare their performance with benchmarks, a reporting practice that helps readers understand the significance of the performance data being provided.

Two of the companies report third-party verification of their GHG emissions data. Two others state that they are working toward third-party verification. Two also describe external audits of climate change issue management. Finally, four of the five companies report that they arrange some form of internal audit of their environmental health and safety management systems on a regular basis.

Summary-A growing number of observers are arguing the importance of oil and gas companies addressing climate change. A report by former Chase Investment Bank, director Mark Mansley, for example, concludes that the hard-line stance on global warming taken by ExxonMobil (Imperial

Oil's parent company) is exposing the company to unnecessary risk and leading it to forfeit valuable opportunities (Mansley 2002).

Each of the companies reviewed for this study recognizes that climate change poses some type of risk to their ongoing sustainability. Each provides a range of information about their policies, strategies, activities and management of these risks. Each is attempting to manage and reduce GHG emissions through improved energy efficiency.

In addition, all but one provides general information about their cautious attempts to explore opportunities to diversify in anticipation of a possible carbon-constrained future. Oil and gas companies disclose this information using different mechanisms, such as sustainability reports, annual reports (including MD&A), annual information forms, corporate Web sites and speeches.

Suncor and Nexen are the only oil and gas companies reviewed that disclose information about climate change risk in their annual information forms (or 10K form, depending on the company).

Mining Sector Disclosure of Biodiversity

Mining activities have significant impacts on land and on biodiversity. Mining companies face various legal obligations to manage issues such as tailings and land reclamation. More generally, however, failure to manage biodiversity issues can be a business risk to extractive sectors. The ability of mining companies to obtain a "license to operate" from the local community-something that is over and above any formal legal obligations-is becoming increasingly important. Among other things, access to new resources is increasingly becoming conditional on addressing heightened concerns about the impacts on neighbouring land and its biodiversity.

The effective management of biodiversity impacts can pose significant challenges to mining companies. Their operations inevitably have direct, adverse impacts on land and biodiversity, and mining companies have little control over where they operate as their location is determined by the placement of the reserves. A recent World Resources Institute report notes that "three quarters of active mines and exploratory sites overlap with areas of high conservation value and areas of high watershed stress" (Miranda et al. 2003).

Following demands for prohibition of extractive activities in protected areas by NGOs such as WWF, the IUCN World Conservation Congress recommended a moratorium on 'all exploration and extraction of mineral resources in specific IUCN Protected Area Management Categories. The International Council of Metals and Mining has been engaged in a dialogue with the IUCN, and has adopted biodiversity as a key issue. International mining companies such as Rio Tinto, Anglo American and BHP Billiton, have agreed 'not to explore or mine in World Heritage properties' (ICMM, 2003). Biodiversity is also one of the next key reporting issue being addressed by the Mining Association of Canada's Towards Sustainable Mining initiative, illustrating its increasing relevance to the mining industry.

In addition to these informal pressures, mining companies face the prospect of future legislation related to issues of access and biodiversity-related liability. The European Union Environmental Liabilities Directive contains references to biodiversity liabilities, and proposes to make operators bear the cost associated with the implementation of measures necessary to prevent or remediate environmental damage as a result of their activities (ISIS 2004). More generally, as implementation of the requirements of the 1992 Convention on Biological Diversity and its various work programs proceed, there may be a trend toward significant new regulations in numerous jurisdictions around the world. Reflecting the importance of biodiversity to the sector, a multi-stakeholder process established under the Global Reporting Initiative has developed specific criteria that it believes companies should address in their public reports (see Figure 3). Also under development is a Mining Sector Supplement that proposes some variations on the indicators below, including specific additional indicators, such as the number/percentage of sites identified that require biodiversity management plans, and sites with plans in place.

Figure: GRI Biodiversity Criteria

Biodiversity	
EN6. Location and size of land owned, leased, or managed in biodiversity-rich habitats.	EN23. Total amount of land owned, leased, or managed for production activities or extractive use.
	EN24. Amount of impermeable surface as a percentage of land purchased or leased.
EN7. Description of the major impacts on biodiversity associated with activities and/or products and services in terrestrial, freshwater, and marine environments.	EN25. Impacts of activities and operations on protected and sensitive areas. (e.g., IUCN protected area categories 1-4, world heritage sites, and biosphere reserves).
	EN26. Changes to natural habitats resulting from activities and operations and percentage of habitat protected or restored. Identify type of habitat affected and its status.
	EN27. Objectives, programmes, and targets for protecting and restoring native ecosystems and species in degraded areas.
	EN28. Number of IUCN Red List species with habitats in areas affected by operations.
	EN29. Business units currently operating or planning operations in or around protected or sensitive areas.

Unlike the oil and gas sector's treatment of climate change, the mining companies reviewed for this project are not yet disclosing details of the risks associated with their biodiversity impacts and their management of those risks. Documents disclosed by Barrick Gold, Falconbridge-Noranda, Inco., Inmet Mining and Teck Cominco were reviewed.

Policy and strategy-While each of the companies discloses an environmental policy, none provides any explicit commitment regarding biodiversity, and only one (Teck Cominco) explicitly addresses land use management in its policies, committing to undertake progressive reclamation of operating and dormant sites. Similarly, none of the five companies reviewed clearly describes a specific biodiversity strategy that sets out the company's key impacts, activities and objectives to drive performance related to biodiversity.

Most commit in general terms to continuous improvement in environmental or sustainability management. Inco commits to continuous improvement in terms of land use practices, including using native species as part of reclamation. Falconbridge-Noranda describes its sustainable development framework with a specific step to restore land to a useable state and ensure integrity.

The company also references the use of the Environmental Excellence in Exploration (E3) guide developed by the Prospectors and Development Association of Canada, which offers guidance on internationally accepted field operations. The report, where this information is disclosed, does not specifically identify that E3 covers aspects of biodiversity.

Each of the five companies reviewed are members of the Mining Association of Canada (MAC). MAC's Towards Sustainable Mining (TSM) initiative has developed Draft Principles that include a commitment to minimizing operational impacts on the environment and biodiversity. Only Barrick and Inmet disclose that they participate in the TSM. The-others refer to their participation in MAC,-but not to TSM specifically.

Although not specifically disclosed by the companies reviewed, each is participating in public reporting of their performance against TSM indicators. These currently include a set of indicators on tailings management systems; indicators specific to biodiversity are under development. Of the five companies reviewed, only Inmet and Falconbridge-Noranda allow their data to be presented by company, rather than just being incorporated into the sector roll-up.

Governance-Consistent with the high priority given to effective environmental management by the mining sector, each of the companies reviewed provides fairly detailed descriptions of the overall way in which the company has allocated accountability and responsibility for environmental issues. However, none explicitly refers to accountability or management responsibilitics for biodiversity.

Several Canadian mining companies have active stakeholder engagement processes, ranging from local, community-based interactions to interactions with specific constituencies, such as Aboriginal groups, to partnerships with national NGOs. As such, most of the companies reviewed disclose information on the importance of stakeholder engagement and provide examples of the various processes in which they are involved.

Nonetheless, only two of the five report on stakeholder engagement processes specifically focused on biodiversity issues. Falconbridge-Noranda describes a process focused on the protection of a particular waterway, and Inco describes its involvement in the "Mining Sector Protected Areas Consultation," an initiative that brought together the mining industry, government and environmental organizations to discuss issues related to biodiversity.

Management systems-Each of the companies discloses information on its environmental risk management systems. Most also describe site-specific environmental management plans. Each describes various mechanisms in place to account for environmental issues in general or to integrate them into key decision-making procedures. Several describe processes for considering environmental priorities (including reclamation) at the start of the project cycle. Most describe their efforts to integrate environmental costs into their accounting processes, and environmental obligations and reclamation into the overall life of the asset.

Teck Cominco specifically describes the integration of biodiversity and wildlife habitat considerations into its site reclamation program, and comments on how new tools have helped to improve this integration. Barrick also refers to habitat stewardship initiatives and wildlife protection programs.

Overall, however, the five companies describe few explicit commitments, procedures and processes that provide confidence that biodiversity is explicitly and systematically integrated into their operations. This contrasts with the detailed disclosure that some multinationals are starting to provide on biodiversity issues.

To handle the issue of elevated levels of metals in the surface soils at its Port Colborne operations, Inco developed the community based risk assessment (CBRA) process, which the company describes as "... a pioneering community-based approach that is designed both to be highly transparent and to allow generous opportunities for public input." The Inco CBRA approach includes specific biodiversity-related issues, such as studies on the quality and diversity of plants and animals in the area.

Each of the five companies reviewed describes training programs, but none provide enough information to enable the reviewer to understand the scope of training and awareness initiatives.

Performance monitoring, reporting and assurance-Four of the companies disclose some type of land use indicator. Inmet does not provide a land use performance indicator, but does disclose its financial liabilities associated with land use and reclamation.

None provides targets related to biodiversity, and none disclose their impacts on protected and sensitive sites or on the types of habitat their activities have disturbed. Barrick is the only company reporting on the impact of its operations on wildlife.

Figure below presents some of the indicators the mining companies reviewed are using to disclose reclamation costs and liabilities in their annual reports. In some cases, these represent leading current practice in the disclosure of risks related to environmental liabilities.

Figure: Mining Company Reclamation Cost and Liability Indicators

Falconbridge-Noranda	Barrick	Inmet	Inco	Teck Cominco
• Reclamation provisions (Falc.) • Reclamation and other environmental provisions (Nor.) • Depreciation, amortization and reclamation expenses (Nor.)	• Amortization and reclamation costs • Reclamation and closure costs	• Reclam-ation costs • Reclamation liabilities	• Remediation, demolition and other related expenses • Operating costs associated with ongoing environmental and reclamation programs • Estimated reclamation and closure costs	• Environmental and reclamation obligations

All of the companies describe various assurance processes. Four describe an internal audit function for environmental issues. Three also describe external audit programs for their environmental management activities, and one (Barrick) describes the third-party assurance process for its environmental report. Inmet discloses a summary of its various audit findings against a rating indicating whether the finding is likely to have an adverse financial impact on the company. Biodiversity is not generally identified as being incorporated into company assurance processes, although Barrick and Inco do disclose audits related to reclamation.

Summary-Each of the companies reviewed emphasizes the importance of environmental issues to its ongoing success. They all describe environmental governance processes; management systems; and performance, monitoring and assurance processes. In general, however, there is only limited disclosure of information on biodiversity risks in the public information provided by the five mining companies reviewed for this study. Indeed, none of them provides a detailed description of how the company assesses the potential significance of the biodiversity issues its faces and how it manages those issues.

This contrasts with the practices of some of the leading multinational mining companies, which are starting to report extensively on biodiversity impacts and management. Leading companies are also demonstrating the integration of biodiversity into internal and external audit protocols, including into ISO 14001 audits as a significant aspect (Insight Investment 2003, p. 31). Canadian companies could consider providing more comprehensive disclosure of information relating to biodiversity, and drawing from biodiversity criteria within the GRI guidelines and sector supplement, where relevant.

Financial Services Sector Disclosure of Environmental and Social Risk Considerations Related to Lending and Project Financing

In 1990, a US court decision related to lender liability raised financial institutions' awareness of the environmental risks related to providing capital. The court found Fleet Bank liable for the environmental contamination that occurred as a result of its lending practices under the Superfund legislation.

Although there have been subsequent amendments to the legislation, this case was the impetus for lenders to start to consider the incorporation of environmental risk into their lending decisions. Similarly, the significant public attention focused on the environmental and social impacts of major development projects-such as the Three Gorges Hydroelectric Power Scheme-also demonstrated to financial institutions the importance of balancing financial interests with social and environmental risks.

In response, multilateral funding agencies such as the International Finance Corporation (IFC) of the World Bank Group have played a significant role in the development of environmental and social lending and investment guidelines.

The Equator Principles (EPs), which draw on IFC guidance, promote environmental and social responsibility in project financing at financial institutions. Several financial institutions around the world, including two of the companies reviewed, RBC and the Canadian Imperial Bank of Commerce, are signatories.

The EPs commit signatory financial institutions to use the leverage of their project financing to influence project design and performance, and to hold clients accountable for meeting environmental and social performance standards. An NGO coalition recently criticized the EP banks for financing projects that do meet EP standards, and for a lack of transparency about implementation of the EPs (BankTrack 2004).

Another initiative that is attempting to raise awareness of non-traditional lending risks (and other issues) is the United Nations Environment Programme Finance Initiative. Among other things, the UNEP FI has produced the Statement by Financial Institutions on the Environment and Sustainable Development. Canada's six largest banks, one investment management company and the national Export Development Corporation have signed the UNEP FI Statement, recognizing that the identification and quantification of environmental risk should be part of the routine process of financial risk assessment and management. A similar statement exists for the insurance industry.

As revised-May 1997

We members of the financial services industry recognize that sustainable development depends upon a positive interaction between economic and social development, and environmental protection, to balance the interests of this and future generations. We further recognize that sustainable development is the collective responsibility of government, business, and individuals. We are committed to working cooperatively with these sectors within the framework of market mechanisms toward common environmental goals.

1. Commitment to Sustainable Development
   - 1.1 We regard sustainable development as a fundamental aspect of sound business management.
   - 1.2 Believe that sustainable development can best be achieved by allowing markets to work within

an appropriate framework of cost-efficient regulations and economic instruments. Governments in all countries have a leadership role in establishing and enforcing long-term common environmental priorities and values.

1.3 We regard the financial services sector as an important contributor towards sustainable development, in association with other economic sectors.

1.4 We recognize that sustainable development is a corporate commitment and an integral part of our pursuit of good corporate citizenship.

2. Environmental Management and Financial Institutions

2.1 We support the precautionary approach to environmental management, which strives to anticipate and prevent potential environmental degradation.

2.2 We arc committed to complying with local, national, and international environmental regulations applicable to our operations and business services. We will work towards integrating environmental considerations into our operations, asset management, and other business decisions, in all markets.

2.3 Wo recognize that identifying and quantifying environmental risks should be part of the normal process of risk assessment and management, both in domestic and international operations. With regard to our customers, we regard compliance with applicable environmental regulations and the use of sound environmental practices as important factors in demonstrating effective corporate management.

2.4 We will endeavor to pursue the best practice in environmental management, including energy efficiency, recycling and waste reduction. We will seek to form business relations with partners, suppliers, and subcontractors who follow similarly high environmental standards.

2.5 We intend to update our practices periodically to incorporate relevant developments in environmental management. We encourage the industry to undertake research in these and related areas.

2.6 We recognize the need to conduct internal environmental reviews on a periodic basis, and to measure our activities against our environmental goals.

2.7 We encourage the financial services sector to develop products and services which will promote environmental protection.

3. Public Awareness and Communication

3.1 We recommend that financial institutions develop and publish a statement of their environmental policy and periodically report on the steps they have taken to promote integration of environmental considerations into their operations.

3.2 We will share information with customers, as appropriate, so that they may strengthen their own capacity to reduce environmental risk and promote sustainable development.

3.3 We will foster openness and dialogue relating to environmental matters with relevant audiences, including shareholders, employees, customers, governments, and the public.

3.4 We ask the United Nations Environment Programme (UNEP) to assist the industry to further the principles and goals of this Statement by providing, within its capacity, relevant information relating to sustainable development.

3.5 We will encourage other financial institutions to support this Statement. We are committed to share with them our experiences and knowledge in order to extend best practices.

3.6 We will work with UNEP periodically to review the success in implementing this Statement and will revise it as appropriate.

We, the undersigned, endorse the principles set forth in the above statement and will endeavor to ensure that our policies and business actions promote the consideration of the environment and sustainable development.

Non-governmental organizations have recognized the influence that financial sector organizations have on business, and have begun to target banks' investment and lending practices. A campaign in the United States, for example, has successfully pressured Bank of America and Citigroup to publicly release policies and commitments on climate change and forest investments.

In Canada, there has been a regulatory driver for improved disclosure of CR information. The Public Accountability Statements Regulations (2002) require banks and other financial institutions with equity of $1 billion or more to publish an annual statement describing their contributions to the Canadian economy and society. Between Stratos' two benchmark surveys on corporate sustainability reporting (2001 and 2003), the number of sustainability reporters in this sector increased sharply from four to 19 (Stratos Inc. 2003, p. 4). Corresponding increases in other sectors were much smaller. In addition, the quality of disclosure by Canadian financial institutions has improved over this period. Another important development is the GRI's release of sector-specific supplement to assist financial institutions in their sustainability reporting practices.

Banks Urged to Disclose Ethical Risks

Canada's big banks received resolutions in 2002 from Real Assets Investment Management Inc. to issue reports discussing the social, environmental and ethical risks "that may significantly affect the company's short and long-term value and how they might impact on the business" and the policies and procedures they have in place to manage these risks. More recently, asset management firms, such as ISIS, have engaged Canada's big five in discussions related to environment and project finance (ISIS, 2004).

As a service industry, banks are keenly aware of the importance of their reputation in their local communities and society at large. Their reputation is also important for employee attraction and retention. European banks and financial institutions, in particular, are engaging more actively in environmental and social agendas. They are also becoming more public about their activities, recognizing that they affect their reputation and, in turn, their client base.

To understand how Canadian banks are responding to the issue of disclosure related to lending and project financing, we looked at five of Canada's largest banking institutions-Bank of Montreal (BMO), Canadian Imperial Bank of Commerce (CIBC), Royal Bank of Canada (RBC), Scotiabank and Toronto-Dominion Canada Trust (TD).

Policies and strategy-All the banks except TD disclose having a general environmental policy that includes specific commitments related to incorporating environmental risk assessment into their lending practices. In addition to their general environmental policies, CIBC, RBC and Scotiabank describe more specific environmental risk lending policies.

Although BMO does not disclose that it has such specific policies, the commitments in its general environmental policy are broader than are those of the other banks. BMO claims that it considers ethical, political, social and economic factors in addition to normal lending considerations, and articulates a position related to financing military equipment purchases.

None of the banks disclose having a strategy in place that sets specific goals or targets related to incorporating environmental and social risks into lending and project financing decision-making. However, both CIBC and RBC are signatories to the Equator Principles, which does provide a framework for the incorporation of environmental and social aspects into large project financing projects. All the banks have well-developed procedures around credit risk.

CIBC and RBC are the only Canadian banks to identify the establishment of specific Environmental Risk Management divisions to analyze environmental risks inherent in lending and investment activities.

Governance-All the banks report that they evaluate environmental risks in lending transactions. However, only CIBC and RBC describe having specific Environmental Risk Management divisions. RBC reports that the mandate of its Environmental Risk Management Group has expanded over time to cover not only environmental credit risk, but also corporate sustainability, new products and reputational risk. All the banks reviewed have senior management committees (often more than one with different responsibilities related to risk management), as well as Board-level committees that oversee risk. Many banks (e.g., TD) also have specific credit and market risk committees-often chaired by the President and Chief Executive Officer-that review large individual credits, industry concentrations and major policy issues involving credit or market risk. All of the banks are fairly clear in disclosing the accountabilities and reporting relationships around risk. CIBC, RBC and BMO provide more explicit descriptions of the various accountabilities for environmental risks related to lending.

The process by which companies develop policies and strategies and manage specific issues is important. Incorporating the views of key stakeholders in this process is increasingly seen as an effective tool to identify and elucidate potential risks and opportunities. Beyond some general information from CIBC about launching an external environment Web site to communicate information (including information on environmental risk), the banks do not disclose information on the engagement of stakeholders related to environmental risk. This is an area that could be improved. At a minimum, one would expect to see information from CIBC and RBC related to engagement based on the Equator Principles.

Management systems-All the banks studied provide reasonably clear descriptions of their processes for managing credit risk, including reporting relationships. RBC, CIBC and BMO are more explicit than Scotiabank and TD in specifically addressing environmental risk management related to lending (in their Public Accountability Statements and Web sites).

None explicitly describe how they incorporate social and ethical risk into management systems, however. Interestingly, in the discussions of credit risk in their annual reports, only CIBC, Scotiabank and BMO explicitly mention environmental risk. This illustrates a lack of integration, on the part of some of the banks, between the information in their Public Accountability Statements and the information in their annual reports, which are their primary financial disclosure documents. Consistency in messaging across different disclosure mechanisms is essential to demonstrate commitment to a specific issue and the extent to which it is integrated into the company's business.

Based on the information reported across the different disclosure vehicles, CIBC and RBC are the most explicit in describing how environmental risk is integrated into lending decisions. However, this process discussion does not specifically address the application of the Equator Principles to large financing projects. Neither bank goes beyond a general commitment to the principles to describe how they implement them.

Only RBC, CIBC and BMO are explicit in outlining the specific environmental risk factors they consider in assessing credit risks. All except Scotiabank describe the different tools they use to conduct environmental evaluations, such as questionnaires, checklists, Phase I Environmental Site Assessments (ESAs) and Phase II ESAs. The type of borrower/business and the size of the loan trigger the use of these different tools. RBC breaks down management system information by credit activities. Scotiabank is the only bank to report a specific example of the integration of environmental factors into lending practices.

All the banks have endorsed the UNEP FI Statement on the Environment and Sustainable Development. Nonetheless, none of them disclose specifically what they have done to meet the UNEP FI commitments. RBC and CIBC also disclose that they are signatories to the International Chamber of Commerce (ICC) Business Charter for Sustainable Development, but similarly do not disclose what they have done to meet the Charter's commitments. Similarly, while Scotiabank and TD disclose that they are involved in the Environmental Issues Group of the Canadian Bankers Association, they do not describe the results of their involvement.

Ensuring that bank employees have the awareness and competence to manage environmental and social risk in their lending decisions is essential to illustrate the bank's effective management of these issues. Only CIBC and BMO specifically describe the training they provide to employees related to the integration of environmental risk into lending decisions. CIBC has created an online training program and specific guidance documents, and BMO has incorporated environmental risk training into a broader skills development program.

Performance monitoring, reporting and assurance-All the banks disclose a fairly standardized set of credit risk indicators (e.g., credit risk concentration, provisions for credit loss). Only CIBC discloses performance indicators specific to the integration of environmental risk into lending decisions. The specific performance indicators used by CIBC include:

- number of credit inquiries determined to be high risk and subject to further evaluation;
- number of credits requiring subsurface investigation to determine presence, degree and extent of contamination;
- number of credits involving sites requiring further action as a result of CIBC's due diligence investigation; and
- number of site inspections and assessments performed by CIBC Environmental Risk Management.

Without access to specific performance data related to how environmental risk is considered in bank lending practices, the capital markets cannot ascertain the degree to which a bank has integrated these considerations into its processes.

Well-developed assurance processes tend to be an indicator of a relatively mature management system. In their discussions of accountabilities, each bank is clear on the oversight function that various committees have to ensure credit risk policies and procedures are being applied systematically and that credit risk is being managed. Only BMO discloses information on the use of internal audits to confirm that it is adhering to its environmental risk guidelines, however.

None of the banks disclose the use of external audits related to environmental credit risk, and none describe the use of third-party verification regarding the environmental credit risk information in their disclosures. Each of the banks describes the use of standard financial statement verification. This would cover overall credit risk data, but it is unclear whether it incorporates environmental credit risk.

Summary-All the banks have policy commitments related to incorporating environmental risk assessment into their lending practices. They all also state that they have standards or procedures in place to assess existing or potential exposure to environmental liability. Some have also signed commitments related to the management of environmental and social risks under various international and domestic initiatives (the Equator Principles, the UNEP FI, the ICC Business Charter for Sustainable Development, and the work of the Canadian Bankers Association's Environmental Issues Group).

Nonetheless, the relatively poor disclosure of performance information limits an investor's ability to assess the extent to which each of these banks is managing environmental risks systematically. And the almost complete absence of information about how they are managing social risks invites the conclusion that they are not addressing this issue in any sort of systematic manner.

Compliance Disclosure Across Sectors

Compliance with legal obligations is critical to the ongoing success of a company. It is also a common criteria or factor used by all segments of the capital markets in assessing quality of management to help inform investment decisions. Non-compliance can result in fines and approval delays. In cases of extreme negligence or deliberate criminal activities, non-compliance can lead to the incarceration of senior executives. Non-compliance incidents can impair a company's reputation and undermine shareholder confidence.

In most cases, compliance entails conforming to applicable domestic statutory and regulatory requirements. Increasingly, however, stakeholders, including some leading investors, are calling on Canadian and other multinational companies operating abroad to comply with Canadian rules in overseas operations where the host country does not have relevant rules of the same rigour.

All of the 15 companies reviewed disclose information on commitments and management systems related to regulatory compliance. In almost all cases, the companies provide much more information about their systems and performance related to compliance with environmental, health and safety (EH&S) legal requirements than with respect to social policy requirements, such as employment equity or human rights.

The five mining companies and five oil and gas companies disclose a similar range of issues related to their EH&S obligations. The five banks differ from their resource counterparts. Instead of managing compliance to regulations related to the direct impacts of their activities, the banks manage conformity with applicable legal restrictions on the types of loans they can make and with policies that guide their lending and investment decisions.

As a result, while the ten resource companies all disclose much of the same type of compliance-related information, the five banks disclose quite a different set of information.

Policies and strategy-All 15 companies have formal policy commitments to meet or exceed relevant legal requirements.

Governance-All also describe either Board-level or senior management oversight and accountability mechanisms related to compliance. All of the resource companies identify and account for the costs of complying with various EH&S compliance obligations, particularly with respect to remediation in the case of mining companies, and air emissions and remediation in the case of oil and gas companies. Most also discuss the potential costs of complying with anticipated new legal requirements.

Management Systems-All ten of the resource companies describe variants of EH&S management systems that are intended, among other things, to ensure compliance with relevant legal obligations. Each of the banks, by contrast, describes management systems for implementing lending guidelines and for dealing with risks such as non-compliance with the Proceeds of Crime (Money Laundering) and Terrorist Financing Act.

Each of the resource companies also describes ongoing training and awareness programs and activities designed to ensure, among other things, that employees are aware of and able to comply with relevant EH&S obligations. Only TD provides any specific information related to organization-wide compliance training, although CIBC identifies that a Legal and Compliance Intranet site is available for employees.

Performance monitoring, reporting and assurance-Each of the resource companies discloses various performance data related to compliance with EH&S regulatory and corporate standards (e.g., percentage compliance with regulatory permits for air and water emissions, fines paid, number of non-compliance events). Inmet, for example, discloses comprehensive information, including the number of convictions, fines, violations and exceedances, as well as reportable spills by site (including closed properties). The company also discloses the number of regulatory inspections undertaken. The banks do not disclose specific performance information as to whether they are in compliance with all relevant legislation.

Each resource company describes programs for internal or external auditing or both. Information from the banks on internal and external audit programs related specifically to regulatory compliance is less comprehensive. TD illustrates best practice reporting by discussing its annual compliance review process, including a letter submitted by the senior management of each business unit stating whether they are in compliance with applicable regulatory requirements, or whether gaps and weaknesses exist. If weaknesses exist, it is disclosed that an action must be established and implemented. BMO is the only bank that discloses the use of external audits of social compliance. BMO states that a Canadian Human Rights Commission audit concluded that the bank is in compliance with all the statutory requirements related to the Employment Equity Act.

Summary-There is a strong focus on compliance, reinforced by detailed disclosure, primarily by the resource companies in this study. The major focus of compliance disclosure is on EH&S issues, rather than on social obligations. Even with respect to EH&S, however, the companies reviewed use a range of indicators, inhibiting efforts to compare performance.

CONCLUSIONS AND RECOMMENDATIONS

Corporate responsibility seeks convergence between creating value for a company and for its stakeholders in environmental, social and economic terms. In the short-term, it can entail the effective management of broader economic, social and environmental impacts and risks in order to reduce costs and enhance a company's reputation. Over the longer-term, it provides business value-addressing CR effectively can mean the prosperity of both the individual company and the society on which it depends-in ongoing access to natural, human and social capital.

The various drivers for CR include:

- Public expectations. Canadian expectations that corporations should act responsibly.
- Stakeholders. Stakeholders may include employees (who must be hired, retained and motivated), communities (which play a critical role in providing an informal "license to operate") and advocacy groups (which have become increasingly effective at using market campaigns such as product boycotts).
- Investor awareness and action.
- Government laws, policies and exhortations.

Currently, awareness of CR issues exceeds the demand for and provision and use of relevant information. The following recommendations focus on options for overcoming that disparity, particularly with respect to the role that capital markets should play in promoting CR.

Materiality is emerging as a central concept in linking the capital markets with corporate responsibility. The interpretation of what is material-information that is considered important in making investment decisions-is expanding rapidly, both through guidance provided by professional associations such as the Canadian Institute of Chartered Accountants, and through the practices of companies in their non-financial (or CR) disclosure.

Building on this, leading Canadian companies in such sectors as chemicals, utilities, and oil and gas are providing information on their CR practices in investor briefings. This is done in cases where CR fits with a company's business strategy-for example, a focus on long-term acquisitions or raising capital in European markets, situations where social and environmental risk factors may be better considered by the markets-or where they can demonstrate their management of concrete risks such as compliance with environmental regulations.

This can build investors' confidence in the company's operations by demonstrating quality management and by providing a real picture of the company's operations.

Recommendations for Capital Markets

Organizations and individuals from the capital markets have sponsored or otherwise been involved in various process that recommend how to gain access to better information about corporations' capacity to manage CR issues, as well as how to better use this information.

The UNEP FI AMWG process identified ten indicators of well-functioning capital markets:

Investors:

- Government and multilateral agency pension funds and their selection consultants integrate consideration of environmental, social and corporate governance (ESC) criteria into their investment mandates.

- Trustees and their selection consultants integrate ESC issues into the formulation of their investment mandates and the selection of investment managers.
- Institutional investors specify ESC guidelines within their proxy voting policies.

Asset managers:

- Asset management firms actively request mainstream brokerage house research on ESC criteria in fundamental analysis.
- Asset management firms have internal ESC research capacity.
- Asset management firms incorporate ESC criteria into their portfolio management process.

Capital markets:

- Brokerage houses are appropriately equipped to integrate ESC criteria into fundamental company analysis.
- Stock exchanges include ESC criteria in their listing and disclosure requirements for companies.
- Accounting standards boards and rating agencies integrate ESC considerations into their frameworks.
- Financial analysts training and certification programs integrate ESC considerations.

Starting this year, the AMWG is planning to use this set of indicators to track global integration of environmental, social and corporate governance criteria into the work of investors, asset managers and capital markets on an annual basis.

Other processes have resulted in similar recommendations, some focused on CR generally, and others focused on specific issues.

For example, the UK Universities Superannuation Scheme (USS) Fund recently sponsored a discussion paper that provided recommendations on the steps institutional managers like USS should take to manage their exposure to investment risks associated with climate change (Mansley and Dlugolecki 2001).

The paper was prepared, in part, by the past President of the UNEP Insurance Industry Initiative. Among other things, it recommends that institutional investors should:

- Review their portfolio's direct property investments for climate change risks and identify measures to mitigate risk exposure.
- Engage with investee companies to encourage them to report on their climate change exposures and the management's response.
- Produce a statement of what the fund considers to be broad principles of good practice for managing climate change risks in investee companies in terms of assessment of climate change risks, corporate strategy and reporting.
- Request that sell-side brokers comment on a company's relative exposure to climate-related risks and the management's capabilities and approach to managing those risks.
- Enhance their own management capabilities for dealing with climate change by undertaking a program of internal awareness-raising and learning.

Building on emerging leading practices by capital market players, as well as the recommendations developed through international initiatives, the following recommendations are put forward to strengthen the demand side of the CR disclosure equation in Canada.

Broadening the Use of International Guidance

Industry associations such as the Canadian Bankers Association could encourage their membership to more broadly integrate such international norms as the Equator Principles into their lending and project investment decisions, as is the case for its leading members. These principles provide a series of risk-based questions to improve the quality of investment analysis.

CR Awareness-Building and Tools

Professional associations such as the Canadian Investment Institute can build their members' awareness of non-traditional financial information related to environmental and social risks, which bears on capital markets investment analysis. This could involve the development of CR risk questions in the form of simple information gathering templates or checklists.

Recommendations for Disclosure by Companies

As the main suppliers of information about their CR goals, management and performance, companies can make important contributions to the improved integration of that information by the capital markets. This section identifies fivc kcy rccommendations.

Full Disclosure of Material Risk

At a minimum, companies need to ensure that they comply fully with existing requirements to disclose all information that is "material" to the company's well-being. Several recent studies have documented a wide disparity in the degree to which companies in the same sectors disclose the same types of environmental risks. The CICA MD&A

guidance document provides information on accounting for such material risks related to environmental and social drivers of the business. Canadian securities regulators' requirements for Annual Information Forms provide further guidance; for example, mining companies must provide information on environmental liabilities. A succinct summary of non-traditional material risk requirements and guidance would make such requirements more transparent to the capital markets and provide guidance on how to disclose such information.

Statement of Business Value

To the extent to which companies are addressing corporate responsibility issues as opportunities and not just as risks to be managed, companies can clearly explain their objectives, strategies and approaches for managing these issues.

For capital markets to begin rewarding companies for pursuing these types of proactive strategies, companies need to demonstrate to the capital markets that the opportunities they are seeking are significant, that they are well positioned and managed to attain those opportunities, and that the opportunities add business value.

Standardized Formats and Metrics Recognized by Analysts

Companies need to ensure that the information they are providing is presented in a form that is useful to the capital markets. For information about CR to meet this test, it needs to have the same, well-understood characteristics as the financial and compliance-related information that publicly traded companies have long generated. One of the key features that is absent at present is consistency or comparability. Several sectors have developed standardized indicators for various aspects of their environmental, health and safety performance. Most of the oil and gas companies reviewed in section 3.2 of this report use standardized metrics for downstream and upstream energy intensity developed either by the Canadian Association of Petroleum Producers or the Canadian Petroleum Producers' Institute.

The development and use of more such standardized indicators to address the full range of CR performance issues relevant to a sector would greatly enhance the degree to which the capital markets are likely to make use of CR information.

Transparency of Performance

Companies need to ensure that they disclose information on both their successes and their challenges, and that they address the same issues in a consistent manner from year-to-year. Disclosures that lack candour will inevitably be suspect, particularly when it addresses a challenging and ill-defined set of issues such as CR.

GRI as an Emerging International Reporting Standard

In their sustainability reports or integrated reports, companies should consider following the international guidelines being developed by the Global Reporting Initiative. The GRI has developed guidance for generic corporate sustainability reporting, and is in the process of developing a series of sector-specific guidance documents.

In a very pronounced trend, the best sustainability reporters internationally are increasingly modeling their reports on the GRI.

In doing so, they are making an effort to ensure that they address a standard set of key issues identified by a concerted multi-stakeholder effort over the past several years. Significantly, analysts at 17 leading GRI firms recently came together to recommend that companies use the GRI as the common standard for expanded reporting (Social Investment Organization 2004).

Public Policy Recommendations

To date, approaches to promoting the incorporation of CR considerations into capital market decision-making taken by governments in Europe, the United States and Canada have mirrored their approaches to social and environmental policies in general. Several European countries have articulated strong government roles that include both clear policy guidance and the growing use of mandatory disclosure requirements. Public policy in the United States has been much less well-defined and more reactive, albeit with examples of concerted shareholder interventions and litigation and some modest legislative reforms. Canada has seen limited industry response to market demands and public pressure, with some tentative government-industry collaboration but no strong policy signals.

Canadian governments could adopt numerous public policy options without necessarily echoing either the US or European models. Other reports have described the wide range of actions Canadian governments could take to stimulate the development of CR in general (smart regulations, procurement policies, etc.). Within that overall set of options, this section describes three categories of actions to promote the incorporation of CR considerations into capital market decision-making.

Stimulate Demand for CR Information

Governments could stimulate demand for CR information by measures such as:

a) Encouraging environmental regulators to communicate information about non-compliances to financial regulators and to the financial community.

b) Supporting efforts to make participants in the capital markets more aware of the links between CR and financial performance.

c) Surveying capital market analysts to determine their current understanding of non-financial risks.

d) Encouraging and supporting the development of guidelines and standards (such as the International Code of Ethics for Canadian Business) that set a benchmark for good performance on which investors, lenders and analysts will expect companies to base their CR disclosure.

e) Enhancing capacity within the capital markets community by helping develop and disseminate analytical tools that can help analysts assess the risks and benefits to which a company is exposed as a result of its particular CR profile.

f) As appropriate, reviewing and revising legal constraints (such as the prevailing interpretations of fiduciary duties) that may impede the willingness or ability of pension and other investment fund managers to account for CR considerations.

Facilitate CR Disclosure

Governments can facilitate CR disclosure through measures such as:

a) Ensuring stricter enforcement by securities regulators of existing environmental disclosure requirements.

b) Providing information to Canadian companies on the business case for implementing CR.

c) Conducting and disseminating market research that helps identify emerging CR expectations, practices and opportunities in various markets that are of interest to Canadian businesses.

d) Enhancing companies-capacity to manage and report CR through training programs and the development, -dissemination and promotion of key tools -such as environmental management systems and social auditing.

e) Helping develop or promote the development and adoption of standardized performance metrics that help companies measure their own performance and benchmark themselves against their peers.

Mandatory Disclosure by Standards

Canadian governments can work in concert with securities exchanges and with standard-setting bodies such as the CICA to raise the bar on expectations and guidance on expected practices for the disclosure and use of financially relevant CR information.

Mandatory CR Disclosure

Finally, governments could consider expanding the scope of legal disclosure requirements. As the UNEP FI recently observed, "governments can reduce barriers to environmental, social and corporate governance analysis by mandating and standardizing the inclusion of these criteria in national and international disclosure frameworks" (UNEP FI 2004, p. 7).

The measures taken through the Public Accountability Statements Regulations for the financial services sector provide one model, as do the social, environmental and ethical disclosure requirements used by pension funds in other countries.

Another approach is to amend the Canada Business Corporation Act with a clear and simple requirement for or reference to the MD&A to be provided to shareholders, in addition to financial statements.

Supply Study Design

The study collected information that corporations in the selected sectors provide to the capital markets through a range of disclosure vehicles. For the agreed sustainability issue in each sector, the types of information collected included:

Policy and Strategy

- *Policy:* The company makes a policy commitment to understand and manage issue risks.
- *Strategy:* A strategy is in place that sets out the company's key impacts, activities and objectives to drive issue-related performance.

Governance

- *Responsibilities:* Accountability and responsibility for issues is assigned at all levels.
- *Stakeholder Engagement:* Engagement from key stakeholders is undertaken to inform understanding of issues and impacts and possible responses.

Management Systems

- *Risk Management:* Management acknowledges the business risks associated with operations and demonstrates that they have reviewed their own operations as a result of this knowledge and identified key areas of risk and impact. Risks related to issues have been factored into risk evaluation for normal business operation and changes in operations. The company has made a commitment to understand and manage its impact.
- *Integration:* Issue risks and opportunities are integrated at key decision-making points, including business planning and risk evaluation, investment

decision-making, business development and projects, operational management, and the assurance process.

- *Site and Facility Level Management:* Issues are managed either through integration of the issues into site management plans or through the development of Issue Action Plans for all sites and facilities.
- *Partnerships:* Evidence of local, national and international partnerships to identify and manage issue impacts and risk.
- *Competencies and Employee Awareness:* Key staff competency is ensured through recruitment or training. Mechanisms are in place to raise the awareness of employees in key positions.

Performance Monitoring, Reporting and Assurance

- *Key Performance Indicators:* The company monitors and reports on its performance and progress in managing risks around issues.
- *Internal Audits:* Internal reviews are conducted on the extent to which issue risks are being managed at all levels of the business.
- *External Audits:* Independent external reviews are conducted on the extent to which issue risks are being managed at all levels of the business.
- *Third-party Verification:* A third party verifies the company's performance and/or reported information regarding issues management.

6

INVESTMENT IN YOUNG AND ESTABLISHED MICROENTERPRISES

INTRODUCTION

Worldwide and particularly in transition economies, the entrepreneurial firm is perceived as an engine of economic growth. Across countries, entrepreneurs face various constraints and must overcome diverse challenges in order to sustain and expand their operations. This paper presents evidence that imperfections in the credit market and insecurity of property rights restrict small firms' investment and growth in Russia.

The ability of entrepreneurs to fund new projects is essential for business expansion. Small firms often face financing constraints because their internal funds are limited, and since small firms find it difficult to signal their quality to investors, external funds are not always available. In Russia, additional restrictions come from the weak institutional framework and numerous legal and regulatory constraints.

Moreover, the supply of external finance is limited, due to the lack of skilled bankers and appropriate lending technologies. Under these circumstances, small firms' investment is often limited to the amount of available internal funds.

Recent studies have explored the degree to which firm size and financial leverage influence the sensitivity of investment to the availability of internal funds in small and medium- sized enterprises (SME) in transition countries. The small firms' financial needs, however, are related to the age of the firm (the financial growth cycle), but this relationship has been largely unexplored. Moreover, the supply of credit is determined by existing lending technologies, and standard banking technology is not friendly to younger firms.

This paper investigates to what degree the investment of small firms of different ages is sensitive to the availability of internal funds, and how does the security of property rights influence this relationship. The analysis concludes with estimation of a credit supply equation, in order to determine whether providers of formal finance are able to resolve problems of asymmetric information and offer sufficient funds to meet the small firms' demands.

METHODOLOGY AND PREVIOUS STUDIES

In a perfect capital market, the investment decision of the firm is independent of the source of finance (Modigliani and Miller, 1958). However, in the presence of transaction costs and asymmetric information, external finance is either rationed or is available at a premium (Stiglitz and Weiss, 1981; Myers and Majluf, 1984).

In such circumstances, external and internal finance are no longer perfect substitutes, and for firms facing high information costs, investment will be limited by the available internal funds (Fazzari et al., 1988). The financing constraint does not affect all firms uniformly, however, and the degree of effective constraint that various firms face provides information on the capacity of the financial system to fund the growth of firms. Fazzari, Hubbard and Peterson (1988) develop an empirical test to distinguish constrained from relatively less constrained firms.

The methodology involves splitting the sample into sub-samples, based on theoretical priors (size, age, financial leverage, and the like), and estimating reduced-form investment equations. Within each sub-sample (fixed) investment is regressed on two groups of variables-investment opportunities and cash flow. A test is then performed to check whether the difference between the estimated cash flow coefficients in the sub-samples is statistically significant. Statistically significant difference is evidence that firms with higher dependence on cash flow for investment face higher information costs and are most likely to be unable to obtain external funds.

Studies have shown that the liquidity constraints that small and medium-size enterprises face in transition countries often differ from those observed in developed economies. In developed countries, the investment of the most informationally opaque firms (smaller, younger) is most sensitive to liquidity constraints (Fazarri et al., 1988). Budina et al. (1999) argue that, in Bulgaria, smaller firms are more liquidity constrained but for reasons different from those suggested by theory.

These authors show that, due to the prevailing soft budget constraints that characterized bank lending, the investment of firms with a significant level of long-term debt (bigger, mainly state-owned firms) was not liquidity constrained, while the investment of firms without debt, as were most of the smaller private firms, showed higher sensitivity to liquidity. Chow et al. (2000) show that smaller firms in China are less liquidity constrained than bigger firms. The authors attribute this to the greater efficiency of smaller firms. Perotti and Gelfer (2000) find evidence that Russian firms with closer ties to industrial-financial groups face lower liquidity constraints than those who do not have ties to the banks.

The institutional structure of the transition process also affects the behavior of small firms. In a weak institutional environment, corrupt government officials and (semi-) criminal organizations influence the security of property rights and thus firms' investment and growth. Johnson et al. (1999) argue that firms will undertake projects with positive net present value only if convinced that they can use the fruits of the investment. If firms' property rights are badly defined and poorly enforced, firms will be less willing to expand and will invest less. These authors develop a pecking order model of investment, and incorporate the specific transition circumstances through an index that reflects the security of property rights.

They show that, prior to 1997, the investment of small firms in Poland, Romania, Slovakia, Ukraine, and Russia was determined primarily by the security of property rights, while availability of internal and access to external funds were less important. Johnson et al. (1999) admit, however, that access to external finance will become important as profit margins decline.

Using 1997 survey data from de novo firms in the Czech Republic, Hungary and Poland, Bratkowski et al. (2000) also find that investment needs are met by the existing financial system. In their study, firms that did not apply for credit were less constrained by the availability of internal funds than was investment in firms that received credit. The authors also study what determines the supply of credit and find evidence that banks play an adequate role in financing small firms' growth, successfully mitigating problems of asymmetric information. Pissarides et al. (2000)

and Lizal and Svejnar (2000), however, provide evidence that the lack of adequate access to external funds has significantly constrained investment in SMEs in Bulgaria and Russia, and the Czech Republic.

Studies of liquidity constraints of firms in transition countries and in Russia have not accounted for the influence of the firm's financial growth cycle.

The Financial Needs of Newly Created small firms may differ from those of older firms; younger firms may find it more difficult to signal their quality to lenders and thus obtain external finance. Moreover, most of the research has been undertaken for SMEs, where small firms hire up to 100 employees and medium firms hire up to 500 employees. Research on very small firms is limited because it is difficult to observe and measure their transactions. This paper adapts the liquidity constraints approach to study the financing constraints of very small firms, with up to 25 employees.

OVERVIEW OF THE FINANCIAL SECTOR

Banking and banks in Russia have a very short history. The Soviet banking sector consisted of a mono-bank system, with a re-distributive function-supplying the planned funds from the public and the Government to enterprises and people. The banking reform of 1992 split up the main sectoral banks (the savings Sberbank, Vnesheconombank, and Agroprombank) into smaller banks. Unlike most transition countries, in Russia a very large number of new, private banks emerged shortly after the start of reform. While, up to 1995, the economy declined by 32 percent, the banking sector grew by 43 percent, and the number of new banks picked at 2,500 in 1995 (Warner, 1997). Evidently, it was profitable to engage in banking activities but lending was not the activity that banks pursued.

Post-soviet banking is characterized by three distinctive periods-from 1992 to 1995, from 1995 to the summer of 1998, and post 1998. During the first period, banks were primarily engaged in channeling the direct lending of the Government to state-owned enterprises and made their profits by paying only a 10 percent annual interest rate for funds, at a time when inflation reached 800 percent. Moreover, banks held more than 70 percent of their assets in non-interest bearing deposits. Cheap credit, however, did not flow to entrepreneurs.

Banks rarely engaged in lending and kept the spread between lending and deposit interest rates broad, because the economic realities provided stronger incentives for other financial activities. For example, banks were allowed to hold foreign assets and profited from direct inflationary rents of servicing foreign transactions as well as from the fees collected as a result of the high demand for foreign currency (Warner, 1997).

The banking reform of 1995 eliminated these sources of profits. Banks, however, found it difficult to collect deposits in the post-hyper-inflationary environment and thus lacked resources to acquire risk evaluation expertise and to develop new lending technologies. Moreover, the proliferation of barter rendered traditional banking services less appealing. Banks earned income by non-lending activities such as trading GKOs (a type of T-bills) and by organizing payment on veksels-financial instruments that enterprises used to extend credit to each other (Commander and Mumssen, 1998).

Poorly designed and badly enforced regulations also impeded the ability of banks to lend. Banks were required to block the clients' accounts if any default on tax payments occurred (Hendley et al., 1998). To reduce both the visibility of their transactions and the banks' access to their accounts, enterprises avoided payments through the banking system. The restrictions on the free transfer of enterprises' funds from non-cash into cash additionally prevented firms from opening and using bank accounts.

These regulations made intermediation almost impossible, because banks could not collect information on their clients' transactions and could not use such information when deciding to whom to lend. At the same time, the central bank failed to curb activities that indeed jeopardized the safety of the banking system.

Prudent lending requires that banks develop and use financial products that match their information processing capabilities, so that the credit risk can be properly handled. Regulators failed to prevent the development of too sophisticated products, such as the infamous forward contracts for foreign currency, for which banks did not have the information processing capability (Roe et al., 1998). When the government defaulted on its GKOs in the summer of 1998, and the currency was devalued, many banks went bankrupt.

The irony of the Russian crisis is that mainly smaller banks, engaged in prudent lending to small and medium-sized enterprises, were able to survive the 1998 financial crisis. Within a year following the August financial crisis, lending was stagnant.

In an environment of low-level of intermediation, lending to smaller enterprises was even less appealing. Many, especially the big banks, found it unprofitable to lend to small and newly established firms. Traditional bank technology requires that a potential borrower presents audited financial statements for the previous three years. Such lending technology is inefficient, because banks do not trust financial statements in Russia. Moreover, younger firms (as were the majority of small firms) cannot satisfy the requirement of three years of financial statements. In developed countries, the credit history of the owner is widely used as an indicator for borrower credibility and managerial skills (Berger and Udell, 1998). Russian bankers, however, find it difficult to evaluate the managerial ability of an entrepreneur. For example, if a firm uses the informal sector's help to enforce its contracts with business partners, banks have no means to evaluate and monitor such "business contracts".

At the same time, anecdotal evidence suggests that both banks and small entrepreneurs used private protection because they did not believe that the formal legal system could enforce their contracts. The higher cost of servicing smaller firms and the absence of a technology to deal with the specific risk kept the price of bank credit in Russia high (Roe et al., 1998).

There are not many alternative sources of formal loans for micro and small businesses in Russia. Government programs to support small businesses are few, and they often primarily provide non-financial services. For example, the Federal Fund for Small Business Support provides mainly technical assistance, as its employees have limited experience with credit evaluation. The Regional Enterprise Support Funds, including the one operating in Samara, provide funding for small entrepreneurs but mainly to entrepreneurs who can invest a significant amount of their own capital. These government programs are capital constrained, tend to fund "priority sectors/activities," and often misallocate resources, as government officials grant credits to friends and relatives. In the more rural areas, mutual credit associations and consumer cooperatives also provide some funds to their members.

Innovative microfinance organizations (MFOs) that lend exclusively to micro and small businesses (Opportunity

International, FINCA, the EBRD Small Business Fund) emerged in the mid-nineties but their influence is limited. MFO arrival is somewhat late because only recently have regulations changed to allow their operations. Overall, the high information costs that entrepreneurs face worldwide is accentuated in Russia by the lack of banking tradition and managerial skills, and by the limited information processing capability of the system.

Moreover, banks operated in a restrictive legal environment, which discourages transparency of entrepreneurial activity and makes credit risk evaluation even more difficult. Alternative formal loans have limited capacity to fund small firms' investment. As a consequence, Russian small businesses have been forced to rely even more on their internal funds for investment.

THE DATA

The data come from a survey of 203 very small enterprises (up to 20 empoyees) in Samara, Russia. The survey was implcmented in August 1999, using a sample obtained from the Statistical Department of Samara Oblast.The database of the Statistical Department is comprehensive, because all entrepreneurs are required by law to register in order to start operations.

The survey covered both individual private entrepreneurs and private companies. The sampling is subject to the usual bias that only surviving firms were surveyed. The firms in the sample are very small with average number of employees is 7.8

(including the owner). Most of the firms are retail businesses, approximately a quarter operate in production and a quarter are in services. Two thirds of the owners hold university degrees, but the share of the younger firms' owners with a university degree is smaller than for the more mature firms. A third of the entrepreneurs indicated that they had specific plans to invest in physical capital in the forthcoming year and approximately a third reported that they faced limited opportunities and would have returned to their previous employment if that were possible.

Russian entrepreneurs identified lack of funds as the main constraint to growth-46 percent reported financing as their most serious obstacle. Markets are the main constraint to grow for 43 percent of the entrepreneurs and direct regulations rank third, with 9 percent of the cases. When asked to rank current problems on a scale of one to four (where 1= least problematic, 2= sustainable, 3=problematic and 4 =most problematic), entrepreneurs ranked only taxes higher than financing.

Corruption and private protection were ranked as least problematic (index of 2 and 1.3, respectively). It seems that financing constraints dominate property rights issues, although this does not mean that businesses do not participate in extra-legal exchanges with government officials or private protection companies.

We did not believe that we could obtain an honest answer if we asked the entrepreneurs directly about their transactions with government officials. To measure the influence of the security of property rights, we asked if the entrepreneurs thought that other businesses pay extra legally to government officials for various permits and for business protection.

More than two thirds of the entrepreneurs reported that they believed that government officials are being paid extra-legally to issue permits and to protect the business. A third of the entrepreneurs also reported that they themselves pay people for protection (90 percent answered this question.). Moreover, about 40 percent believe that government officials can change and re-interpret rules concerning individual tax obligations.

The combination of data on extra-legal payments and the ranking of constraints to growth seem to suggest that, after several years of changes, businesses have adapted to the environment and have colluded with government officials in establishing some basic security of property rights, which allow businesses to function.

Bad laws serve a country best when badly enforced, because they allow the most efficient small firms to pay the fee and do their business, as suggested by the theory of the second best applied to small firms in Russia. The evidence also shows that younger firms rely more on private protection, while older firms rely more on extralegal transactions with government officials.

EMPIRICAL SPECIFICATIONS

The empirical model is constructed after Fazzari, Hubbard and Peterson (1988). The sample is first split into two sub-samples-younger firms (age less or equal to 3 years) and older firms (age more than 3 years). We test whether the availability of internal funds influences the firms' decision to invest in fixed capital.

This specification captures the influence of the financial growth cycle, and is allows us to check whether the existing lending technology is biased against younger firms. In addition, the sample is split into micro (with less than 5 employees) and small firms (with 5 up to 35 employees) to study how size may influence investment sensitivity to cash flows.

The biggest challenge in studying micro and small entrepreneurs' investment is to distinguish between business and family assets. Any measure of the level of investment may be incorrect because it is not always possible to separate the physical capital that entrepreneurs use for private purposes from that used for business purposes.

Furthermore, Russian entrepreneurs do not have any incentives to correctly represent their assets and the level of investment. On the contrary, pilot tests revealed that questions about the level of investment were systematically not answered. This problem is resolved here by the use a qualitative dependent variable (as in Johnson et al, 1999), which in a sense "endogenizes the scale".

Instead of a linear regression, we estimate a tobit model to establish whether a firms' decision to invest in fixed assets can be explained by investment opportunity and availability of internal finance. The dependent variable takes the value of one if the firm has specific plans to invest in fixed capital in the following year, and zero otherwise.

Employment growth is the variable used as a proxy for investment opportunities. An alternative is to use the change in sales as in many sales accelerator models. However, Anderson and Kegels (1997) and Grosfeld and Nivet (1997) have argued that in transition countries such backwards looking variables as sales are not an appropriate proxy for the expected profitability of investments. Bratkowski et al. (2000) have also maintained that sales growth is especially inappropriate for start-ups because those can have excellent investment prospects but their sales record would not be impressive.

Bratkowski et al. (2000) and Johnson et al. (1999) use employment growth as a proxy for investment opportunities as in the present empirical specification. The variable that captures the cash flow influence is a dummy that takes the value of one if the entrepreneur indicated that he/she has positive cash flow.

Estimation of probability that a firm will invest in fixed capital is augmented by variable(s) that represent the security of property rights.

The index of property rights mirrors the index used by Johnson et al. (1999). It has a value of 0 if the entrepreneur has answered that he must pay extra legally for protection to informal groups, and to government officials for permits and business protection.

The index has value of 3 if the entrepreneur does not pay for private protection, and believes that businesses do not pay extra legally to government officials for permits and businesses protection. In Johnson et al. (1999) value of zero stands for least secure property rights while value of three measures most secure property rights.

Their index captures "security" of property rights when the legal system and institutions function normally and protect the property rights of businessmen. We argue, however, that in a weak institutional structure and property rights get "secured" through extralegal payments. A negative significant coefficient of the index of security of property tight, therefore, would be interpreted as evidence that bribes actually secure entrepreneurs property rights.

To control for the discretionary power of officials on taxes we use a dummy. It takes the value of one if the entrepreneur has indicated that he believes tax authority have discretionary power to change individual tax obligations and zero otherwise.

To gain additional information on the possibility that in the formal credit market younger and smaller firms are more rationed we estimate a tobit model of credit supply, following Bratkowski et al. (2000). The dependent variable is one if the applicant received a formal loan and zero if the applicant was denied a formal loan. The sample consists of only those firms that have applied for formal credit so that identification is achieved. A self-selection bias may exist because entrepreneurs who believe they cannot obtain a formal loan have not applied.

The explanatory variables in the credit supply equation must affect only credit supply but not investment in order to achieve proper identification of the effect of credit constraints on investment. Prudent lending requires that banks fund profitable projects and guard against unexpected events by requiring collateral. Employment growth is used as a proxy for profitability of the project.

The data set does not contain information on the availability of collateral, but collateral can alleviate asymmetric information problems only if the lender can promptly repossess and resell the asset to recuperate the loss. In Russia, however, very few physical assets can serve as collateral.

For example, only in specific circumstances can apartments serve as collateral (Nadolnyak and Hartarska, 1999). Furthermore, since it is expensive and time consuming to seize collateral, and since reselling the assets on underdeveloped secondary markets is not always possible, banks in Russia are forced to use other methods to guard against losses.

Russian entrepreneurs often manipulate their financial statements therefore lending based on financial statements would not be prudent. However, Russian firms that use the banking system to pay suppliers and to receive payments from clients have established a record that banks can use to evaluate borrowers' credibility. Moreover, by using the banking system firms signal that they are better quality clients because such firms risk having their assets frozen if they are unable to meet tax obligations.

Finally, firms that actively use the banking system are de facto providing collateral, as the funds in their accounts will be seized in case of default. A dummy that takes the value of one if the borrower has actively used his bank account and zero otherwise is used to measure whether banks have used firms' payment record to guard against default.

In developing countries, banks often use the personal credit history of the owner of the business when deciding who gets credit (Berger and Udell, 1998). We use the entrepreneurs' age and education level as a proxy for entrepreneurial abilities.

THE RESULTS

Both investment opportunities and cash flow have a positive and significant effect on the probability that a firm will invest in fixed assets when sub-sampling is done according to age. Significant Chi-squared confirms that the approach is appropriate.

Models one and two show that younger firms with internal funds are 60 percent more likely to invest than are younger firms who do not have internal funds. Older firms with internal funds are 40 percent more likely to invest than are older firms without internal funds.

Clearly, the investment decision is linked to internal capital and the information costs that younger firms face are higher than the information costs that older and more established firms face. Overall, investment in younger firms is 20 percent more dependent on the availability of internal capital than is investment in older firms.

The difference between the coefficients on the cash flow variable is statistically significant. The security of property rights has a non-uniform influence over the investment decision of small firms in Russia. Older firms' decision to invest is affected by the security of property rights but the index of security of property rights in insignificant in the investment equation for younger firms. These results are technically contrary to what Johnson et al. (1999) found.

However, these authors use data from the earlier stages of the economic transition, when profit margins were high and there was a lack of information regarding the bribe practices of various government officials and private "protection firms".

The more people ("institutions") entrepreneurs had to bribe, the more discouraged they became regarding the future of their business and invested less. This is well captured by the security of property rights index where more "secure" property rights means paying to a smaller number of officials. Unlike in 1996, in 1999 Russian established businesses were well aware of the extra legal prices charged by various government officials and private protection people.

Therefore, the more extralegal "relationships" older firms secured through extra legal payments, the more likely were they to invest and expand the business. In this sense, the results here confirm the suggestion of Johnson et al. (1999) that it is the insecurity regarding the incidence of extra legal payments, not the need to pay extra legally that affects firms' investment decision.

For younger firms, however, the need to grow may outweigh concerns of property rights security as shown by the insignificant coefficient on the index of security of property rights.

Taxes rank highest within the group of current problems, and 40 percent of the entrepreneurs believe that tax authorities have the discretionary power to reinterpret individual tax obligations. Surprisingly, however, the dummy for discretionary power of government officials is insignificant in firms' investment equations.

This result only strengthens the conclusion that the necessity to bribe per se does not deter investment. Industry controls show that in both groups retail businesses do not plan to expand their activities, while younger firms operating in both retail and services have limited investment opportunities.

The results from the credit supply equation suggest that lenders were not successful in identifying the best investment projects because profitability, at least as proxied by average employment growth, did not influence who did or did not receive credit.

Moreover, unlike lenders in developed countries who extensively use the main owners' personal characteristics as a measure of borrower credibility, banks in Russia were unable to distinguish entrepreneur's type, at least not if management abilities can be proxied by managers' age and education.

Banks, however, attempted to guard against default by lending to firms who actively used the banking system for their business transactions and who built a payment history. The upshot is that small businesses who did not want to have their activities transparent by using the official payment system had very limited access to formal loans and had to limit their investment to the amount of internal sources or informal loans.

Age is not significant in the credit supply equation. Nevertheless, it may only appear that banks did not discriminate on the basis of age, because this result may be due to a self-selection bias-younger firms, aware that they can not get a formal loan did not even apply. Size played a role in the supply of credit but bigger firms had only a- slight advantage.

Finally, banks did not believe that the service industry offers good returns to investment, so projects in services were generally not funded.

CONCLUSIONS

Research on the financing constraints of very small firms is scarce because it is difficult to observe and measure very small firms' transactions. This paper contributes to the literature by studying the relationship between firm age and liquidity constraints.

The liquidity constraint model is adapted to the specific circumstances of small firms in Russia, and the process of economic transition is added through an index of security of property rights. We find evidence that investment in small firms is strongly influenced by the availability of internal capital.

Overall, younger firms' investment is 20 percent more dependent on internal capital than is investment in older firms. The security of property rights influences investment only in more mature firms. The more extralegal relationships older firms had "secured" through extra legal payments, the more likely they were to invest and expand the business.

The upshot is that insecurity regarding the incidence of extra legal payments, not the need to pay extra legally affects firms' investment decisions. Results also show that for younger firms the need to grow the business outweighs property rights concerns. The formal financial sector did not channel funds to the most successful investment projects but there is evidence that loans were given to firms that had more transparent transactions.

REGENTS PROFESSOR AND STILES PROFESSOR OF AGRICULTURE

This Bulletin discusses the role of information technology (IT) in agricultural lending, particularly in view of the globalization of economic and financial relationships in recent years which brings with it additional risks and uncertainties. It particularly underscores the need for an early warning system for agricultural loans and the incorporation of this information into decisions regarding individual loan requests and portfolio management strategies. The concept of stress testing is combined with a proposed early warning system based upon generally accepted economic concepts to quantify the probability of cash flow stress for benchmark enterprises. This stress will be related to the probability of the borrower covering his/her operating costs and total costs, and the implications for the exposure to credit risk and portfolio risk. This system can be seen as an extension to quantitative history-based credit scoring models currently used by lenders, and can be enhanced to include the probability of default.

7

ROLE OF INFORMATION

INTRODUCTION

Information has traditionally played a major role in lending decisions. The manner in which this information is stored, accessed, and analyzed, however, has changed markedly over the last ten years. Information technology has played a major role in this transformation. Largely gone are the days where lending decisions were made by a loan committee based upon hard copy documents stored in file cabinets.

Internally maintained electronic databases, coupled with acquisition of a borrower's credit history from external credit repositories and credit scoring models, have revolutionized the loan decision-making process. The result is a more efficient decision process, both in terms of the resources required to make the decision, and the time interval necessary to provide the decision to the borrower. But are we using information technology to its fullest potential? And are existing computer-generated credit scores sufficient basis for reaching a decision?

Evaluation of a borrower's credit worthiness has typically rested upon historical information gleaned from credit bureau reports, credit scoring models, and current financial statements. The underlying assumption often voiced is that if the borrower could make payments on schedule in the past, then he/she must represent good future credit risk as well. Many credit scoring models in use today, however, have yet to be tested in a depressed farm economy absent of huge government subsidies.

These models are based upon weights assigned to specific risk factors reflecting how well the applicant did in servicing existing debt commitments during a specific historical time period when government subsidies made the difference between profit and loss.

Agricultural lenders, however, should account for likely future economic trends as well as historical performance when evaluating loans, particularly loans involving the purchase of fixed assets that have little or no alternative use in other sectors, and typically decline in market value during economic downturns.

The globalization of economic and financial relationships in recent years brings with it additional risks and uncertainty. When coupled with the unique risks facing agricultural lenders, the use of historical information is still necessary, but is no longer sufficient.

The evolving agricultural lending environment raises serious doubts as to whether past term debt repayment performance is a good predictor of future debt repayment capacity. The argument applies to the bank's entire current agricultural loan portfolios as well. There is a substantial difference in the behavior of risk factors evaluated during normal business conditions, and the behavior of these factors during financial crises.

Risk to a financial institution manifests itself in a variety of ways, including interest rate risk, liquidity risk, investment risk, operating expense risk, collateral risk, and credit risk, to name a few. The focus of this paper is upon early signals of credit risk, and the implications for specific segments of the bank's portfolio. Specifically, this paper underscores the need for an early warning system for agricultural loans and the incorporation of this information into decisions regarding individual loan requests and portfolio management strategies.

The concept of stress testing is combined with a proposed early warning system based upon generally accepted economic concepts to quantify the probability of cash flow stress for benchmark enterprises. This stress will be related to the probability of the borrower covering his/her operating costs and total costs, and the implications for the exposure to credit risk and portfolio risk.

This system can be seen as an extension to quantitative history-based credit scoring models currently used by lenders, and can be enhanced to include the probability of default. It represents a means to mitigate future credit and supervisory risk.

RELIANCE ON HISTORICAL INFORMATION

Three types of information typically support a lender's evaluation of a borrower's future debt repayment capacity:

* (1) Historical financial indicators derived from previous annual financial statements are used along with information from credit bureau reports to assess the overall historical financial performance of the borrower. These indicators focus on past trends in the borrower's liquidity, solvency, efficiency, profitability and timeliness of loan payments. The credit bureau reports ignore information on the borrower's assets and profitability.

* (2) Comparative financial indicators available from public and private sources, or from internally developed benchmarks, help evaluate a firm's

financial performance relative to other firms operating in the same industry. These indicators are often compared to the institution's underwriting standards to assess the creditworthiness of the borrower when applying for the loan and, in many cases, are used to price the loan.

* (3) Credit scoring models, like the FICO scores available from Fair/Issacs, are based upon historically-determined weights assigned to specific historical factors, and are widely used to separate good loan applications from potential problem loans in the consumer lending and home mortgage lending markets (Hubbard and Gregg 2001). Their principal focus is on how well the applicant did in servicing existing debt commitments during a specific historical time period.

It is important at this point to clearly state that there is absolutely nothing wrong in reviewing a borrower's past loan payment record and how a set of financial indicators have either trended over time or stack up against similar firms. Historical and comparative analysis is important. Furthermore, credit scoring models have merit, although these models as applied in agriculture typically:

(a) place more weight on equity than cash flows,

(b) do not differentiate between sources of income and their potential variability, and

(c) do not incorporate analyses of future profitability and debt coverage.

The "missing link" in traditional quantitative credit analysis therefore is not the coverage of historical information, but rather the almost complete lack of forward information utilized in the process. This is particularly important for longer-term strategic borrowing and lending decisions.

Too much has changed and will continue to change in global agricultural markets to rely solely on the "rearview mirror" approach to lending when going down the road with a borrower. Lenders need to look out the "windshield" as well to see where their farm customers are going and what key forks in the road may mean for problem loan exposure.

This requires the stress testing of plausible magnitudes associated with risk factors affecting borrower behavior and performance. These factors include changes in macroeconomic policy at both home and abroad, changes in international trade policies, changes in domestic farm commodity policy, and trends in global production and consumption patterns. These sources of stress will ultimately affect domestic commodity prices for crops and livestock, and hence the term debt repayment capacity of farm borrowers.

REGULATORY PERSPECTIVES

Regulators of farm lending institutions are aware of the need to stress test debt repayment capacity. During the height of the economic uncertainties facing U.S. agriculture in the late-1990s, the Office of the Comptroller of the Currency, the agency of the U.S. Treasury with responsibility for regulating and supervising national banks, issued a handbook to guide the actions of bankers and examiners in assessing credit risk associated with agricultural loans. As a part of this guidance, examiners were urged to take historic, current and prospective economic conditions into account when assessing the longer-term quality of agricultural loans. It also urged bankers to fully understand and actively manage their agricultural portfolios.

The Farm Credit Administration (FCA), an agency with the responsibility of regulating and supervising the banks and associations that comprise the Farm Credit System in the U.S., included language in their examination manual that urged member associations in a rapidly changing and competitive lending environment to manage their loan portfolios proactively. Both documents point to the need to monitor a variety of external factors that may affect future credit quality.

The phrases "prospective economic conditions", "longer-term quality of agricultural loans", and "manage their loan portfolios proactively" are key phrases that signaled a realization that economic conditions in agriculture are affected by a variety of external risk factors that require ongoing analysis. It is significant that both documents underscored the need to combine historical analysis with pro forma analysis in assessing credit risk at the account and portfolio levels in an increasingly uncertain agricultural lending environment.

WHAT IS AN EARLY WARNING SYSTEM?

Rose (1995) states that "Not only is it useful to look at historical data in a source and uses of funds statement, but it is also extremely important to estimate the business borrower's future sources and uses of funds and its statement of financial position".

It was also suggested that a lending institution would be well advised to carry out a simulation analysis of the customer's future financial condition, assuming an array of different environments, and seeing what the consequences are for the business's pro forma balance sheet, income statement, and sources and uses of funds statement. Rose (1995) further states that "Armed with this information, the loan committee can move toward a more satisfactory credit decision based on its assessment of the most likely future conditions."

Fraser; Gup and Kolari (1996) state that "Analyzing past financial data may not be adequate to make determinations about a borrower's ability to pay back loans in the future." They argue that, "By evaluating the current financial condition and using pro forma statements and sensitivity analysis, credit analysts have a better estimate of the borrower's ability to repay a loan."

The design and implementation of an early warning system should embody the pro forma stress testing efforts referred to above. The system should look at the probability of cash flow stress for key enterprises over a multi-year forecasting interval rather than a multi-year historical interval. In other words, today's portfolio and loan applications should be evaluated for their risk potential over the next five years, say, rather than the last five years. This is the time interval over which loan payments will be made.

What does an early warning system for agriculture look like? Can economic theory give us a hand in designing the system? What do we want the system to tell us? And how do we validate the early warning system once it has been estimated?

PROPOSED EARLY WARNING SYSTEM FOR AGRICULTURE

The foundation of an early warning system for future nonperformance should rest on generally accepted economic principles. This section discusses the procedures for developing an early warning system for agricultural loans and portfolios in the United States.

ECONOMIC FOUNDATION

Economic theory of the firm suggests that the breakeven (zero accounting profit) for the firm occurs where marginal revenue is equal to marginal cost. Average profit per unit of output (P3 _ ATC) at Q3 would be equal to zero. The farm would just cover its total cash costs at P2 by producing quantity Q2, and would just cover its variable costs (costs that vary with the level of production) by producing quantity Q1 if the price fell to P1.

The prospect of a zero net cash income (the price of the commodity is less than P2 when the farmer is producing Q2) implies the enterprise cannot contribute to the farm's ability to cover its scheduled principal payment in the current year.

And if the price is less than P2, the firm cannot meet its total cash costs, which includes scheduled interest payments. In both cases, the farmer also is not covering the depreciation of productive assets, which has longer run implications for the soundness of the loan.

The design of the early warning system for agriculture proposed in this paper is built upon the cost concepts illustrated. The focus of this system is on the key commodities in the agricultural loan portfolio, and the primary commodity in the farmer's operations.

Rather than simulate each and every loan in the portfolio or each loan application, benchmark farms representing the typical cost structure for different sizes and locations of commodities in the bank's agricultural loan portfolio can be used to identify specific enterprises likely to experience cash flow stress over the foreseeable future.

DEVELOPMENT OF SYSTEM

We can begin to develop an early warning system for agricultural loans and portfolios in the United States by using cost of production budgets for specific commodities assembled by extension economists in each state at the sub-state level. The state of Texas, for example, is segmented into 12 production districts. Cost of production budgets for major commodities produced in each of these Texas districts are available for different sizes of operations. This helps capture the effects of economies of size in the cost of production.

These historical budgets, expressed on an average per acre or per head basis, can be updated with projected unit input costs for fuel and other inputs over a forecasting interval.

Similarly, the commodity price can be projected over the same forecasting interval by modeling the factors affecting demand and supply. Thus, rather than observing past prices and average cost of production when assessing accounting profit, one can project these observations over a desired time interval.7 Taking both projections together, we can determine whether or not an enterprise is projected to cover its cash cost of production.

PROBABILITY OF COVERING COSTS

The approach taken in this paper is to project the commodity prices and unit input costs based upon random values for the exogenous variables in the econometrically estimated equations. Simulation of a multi-market set of simultaneous equations would capture the correlation or relationship between the commodities and inputs (Penson and Taylor 1992).

Use of a random number generator to assign values in the exogenous variables over a sufficient number of observations would permit derivation of a cumulative density function (CDF), illustrating the probability that the benchmark farm will not be able to cover its cash operating costs (net cash income is negative) and its total costs (net income is negative). For example, suggests that an enterprise is in a strong position to cover its cash operating costs since the right-hand CDF for coverage of operating costs lays far to the right of zero.

The benchmark farm will contribute $170 per acre to debt repayment capacity from a cash flow perspective. However, the left-hand CDF for coverage of total costs shows there is roughly a 20 percent probability that the enterprise will not be able to cover its total accounting costs in 2005.

The closer the right-hand CDF for coverage of operating costs is to zero, the greater the current cash flow stress for the enterprise, the greater the cash flow stress for the farmer, and the greater the credit risk exposure for the lender. Once this process has been repeated for all the primary commodities in the bank's agricultural loan portfolio over a forecasting interval (say 2005-2010), the bank's portfolio database can be sorted by primary commodity of all borrowers (or at minimum all borrowers with a large exposure or debt outstanding) in specific locations.

This would show the amount of loans outstanding associated with each primary enterprise. Those enterprises with CDFs lying near or to the left of zero have a high probability of experiencing cash flow stress in the near future, and should be closely monitored.

One can also determine the percentage share of the portfolio likely to be under increasing risk over time. For example, if a loan portfolio with $4 billion contains 15 percent of loans where wheat is identified as the primary commodity and the CDF for benchmark wheat farms indicates a high probability of building cash flow stress over the next five years, the early warning system would indicate potential cash flow stress associated with $600 million in current loans.

A proactive bank management team can take steps to deal with this potential problem by:

(1) rationing the quantity of loans made to wheat farmers,

(2) charging a risk premium on long term loans to wheat farmers to compensate for the impending risk,

(3) requiring additional security when making loans to wheat farmers, or

(4) all of the above (Penson 1998).

Regulators, armed with the same information, are more apt to begin examining large loans to wheat producers with a debt-to-asset ratio above levels known to result in nonperformance (Penson 1998).

Validation of the early warning system can be accomplished by back casting over a recent historical period. This would demonstrate how well the system did in identifying portfolio segments that actually came under increased financial stress and needed restructuring of their existing debt, and hence represented a heightened credit risk to lenders.

EVENT STRESS TESTING

The Basel Committee on global financial system defines stress testing as "a generic term describing the various techniques used by financial forms to gauge the potential vulnerability to exceptional but plausible events."

The new Basel Capital Accord mentions that banks adopting an internal rating based (IRB) approach for calculating capital requirements must undertake sound stress testing procedures which "should involve identifying possible events or future changes in economic conditions that could have unfavorable effects on a bank's credit exposures and assessment of the bank's ability to withstand such changes."

This same system can also be used to evaluate the effects of a specific event in the magnitude, for example, of the Asian financial crisis in the late 1990s (Penson,1999; 2000). Examples include what might happen if a substantial outbreak of mad cow disease occurred in the United States or if the soybean rust outbreak in Brazil resulted in bank failures in Brazil and hence, in nonperforming loans at U.S. banks.

While these events might not eventually occur, bank management and regulators would know more about the ability of the entire portfolio to perform under specific stressful conditions. Analysis of external factors through stress testing can help management assess the downside risk associated with the future debt repayment capacity and the ability of existing underwriting standards to correctly separate potential good loans from bad loans.

The goal of an early warning system is to recognize potential cash flow stress and adverse credit risk signals before actually making the loan or, in the case of an existing borrower or portfolio segment, before it is too late to take proactive measures.

PROBABILITY OF DEFAULT

An enhancement to the early warning system proposed above would involve projecting the probability of default or nonperformance for a specific segment of the portfolio (e.g., borrowers with wheat as their primary commodity). Based upon historical observations of nonperformance (e.g., loan volume past due by 90 days or more) by primary enterprise and location, one can econometrically estimate the relationship between this loan volume and net cash income for the primary enterprise along with other variables, including data from credit report bureaus mentioned earlier. One can then generate a CDF for the probability of loan default based upon random events affecting the enterprise's net cash income over a forecasting interval.

Those portfolio segments with a high probability of default would thus require closer attention along the lines suggested above for the early warning system (quantity rationing, price rationing, and/or additional security of loans). Those portfolio segments with a low probability of default would represent potential marketing opportunities. An accurate forecast of the probability of default will also help bank management determine the appropriate level of loan loss reserves.

SUMMARY AND CONCLUSIONS

The information technology revolution, coupled with the gains in efficiency gained in loan approval processes, make the development of an early warning system and event stress testing possible. An early warning system can help management identify pockets of potential risk in time to be proactive in its lending and portfolio decisions. Major regulators in the United States, including the Federal Reserve System, the Federal Deposit Insurance Corporation, and the Office of the Comptroller of the National Bank Administration, all have early warning systems of one type or another that focus on bank portfolios as a whole.

The particular features of the system recommended in this paper are designed specifically for agricultural loan portfolios at the bank level. At a minimum, such a system should be based upon generally accepted economic concepts, be pro forma or forward looking rather than historical in nature, capture the correlation among enterprises, and be validated before it is implemented. Extension to capture the probability of default is recommended where data are available.

Agricultural lenders in the United States have avoided greater levels of nonperforming loans due to the levels of government subsidies to farm -program participants. Government payments as a percentage of net farm income reached as high as 60 percent during the financial crisis besetting U.S. agriculture in the 1980s, and approached nearly 50 percent in the late 1990s. The potential for more restrictive government spending limits in light of the current federal budget deficits underscores the need for an early warning system like that proposed in this paper to warning against future credit and supervisory risk.

Finally, advances in information technology permit more streamlined approaches to loan and portfolio analysis than were practiced in previous generations. The application of this technology, however, requires that banks gather the necessary data from borrowers and other sources to fully utilize its potential. The design of the agricultural loan database and supporting databases should contain current data on the economic performance of borrowers if lenders are to successfully deal with the many risks faced in a rapidly changing global economic environment.

8

UNIVERSAL BANKING-THE INDIAN PERSPECTIVE

Ever since the financial sector reforms were introduced in early 90's the banking sector saw the emergence of new generation private sector banks.

These banks gained at most popularity as they have technology edge and better business models when compared to public sector banks and the most important thing is they are able to attract more volumes simply because they meet their customers requirements under one roof.

If the newer players can do that then why cant the bigger players like the Development Financial Institutions (DFIs) try their hands on it? Here comes the concept of universal banking, its emergence, merits and related issues.

The paper focuses on understanding the concept of universal banking in India and attempts to explain the regulatory role, regulatory requirements, key duration and maturity distinction and lastly the optimal transition path.

The paper also gives an overview of the international experience and argues in favour of developing a strong domestic financial system in order to compete in the global market.

THE CONCEPT

Universal Banking, means the financial entities-the commercial banks, DFIs, NBFCs,-undertake multiple financial activities under one roof, thereby creating a financial supermarket.

The entities focus on leveraging their large branch network and offer wide range of services under single brand name. Universal banking generally takes one of the three forms:-

a. In-house Universal banking. Eg. Germany

b. Through separately capitalized subsidiaries. Eg. England.

c. Operations carried through a holding company. Eg. USA. (Nair, 1998)

Universal Banking includes not only services related to savings and loans but also investments. However in practice the term 'universal banks' refers to those banks that offer a wide range of financial services, beyond commercial banking and investment banking, insurance etc. It is a combination of commercial banking, investment banking and various other activities including insurance. If specialised banking is the one end universal banking is the other. This is most common in European countries.

A narrow view of Universal banking could be activities pertaining to lending plus investments in bonds and debentures. A broader view could include a basket of all the financial activities including insurance. Though the concept is prevalent in countries like France, Germany and USA but is yet to take-off, officially in India.

INTERNATIONAL SCENARIO

Federal Republic of Germany, Switzerland are generally known to be the home of universal banking. Factors like technological up gradation, wide spread of applications, increasing competition in financial sector etc., are the driving forces in-these nations. In few other European countries, almost all other banking and non-banking services are carried out by financial institutions.

For instances, in Germany, commercial and investment banking activities are performed by a single entity, but separate subsidiaries are required for other activities. In UK a separate subsidiaries of commercial banks involve in providing wide range of activities.

What the USA follows is an extreme model, where the commercial banks are prevented legally from combining their normal lending functions with investment operations, where they are separated by several legislative acts, including the Glass-Steagall Act of 1933 and the bank Holding company Act of 1956.

However, at present USA is having a re-look at the position. Much of the international debate on universal banking has been centered around the restriction on diversification of the type.

INDIAN SCENARIO

Commercial Banks

In early 90's the financial sector in India was crying out for reforms. Ever since the process of liberalization hit the Indian shores, the banking sector saw the emergence of new-generation private sector banks. Public sector banks which played a useful role earlier on are now facing deterioration in their performance.

For very long, the banks in India were not allowed to have access to stock markets. So their dealing in other securities were minimal. But the financial sector reforms changed it all, Indian banks started to deal on the stock market but their bitter experience with scams, they became averse to deal in equities and debentures. Off late, commercial banks in India have been permitted to undertake a range of in-house financial services. Some banks have even setup their own subsidiaries for their investment activities. Subsidiaries include in the area of merchant banking, factoring, credit cards, housing finance etc.

Financial Institutions

DFIs were traditionally engaged in long term financing, as their main objective was to take care of the investment needs of industries and to contribute to a better industrial climate.

They had, over the time, built up expertise in merchant banking, project evaluation and also started giving working capital finance. Recently, they were allowed to accept medium-term deposits within the specified limits. Lots of changes have taken place in DFIs in the recent past. Most of DFIs have floated banks, institutions and mutual fund subsidiaries. Ownership changes took place, several institutions went public, organization structure itself got transformed.

INDIAN PERSPECTIVE ON UNIVERSAL BANKING

Some argue that the approach is very slow, while some call for steady approach. The debate of universal banking is very much on. Should India have universal banking and if so when? Much has been written about it domestically, however the following are the issues which are key in Indian context.

i. Regulatory burden

ii. Regulatory requirements

iii. Distinction between maturity and duration

iv. Optimum Transition path

Regulatory Burden

One of the major problems associated with universal banking is the issue of regulation. DFIs in India are governed by separate Acts and banks are regulated by RBI and Banking Regulation Act. DFIs in India have commercial banks as their subsidiaries, but due to the separation of regulation, the DFIs cannot have direct access to the resource base of its subsidiary bank. Without any doubt, the net regulatory burden for all participants in the entire financial system should be equalized in order to ensure that no participant might end up having a disadvantage relative to any other.

The importance of this point can be highlighted by citing the example of USA, Japan, West Germany and Britain where there was a tremendous decline in the share of banks in composition of household financial assets and its movement to mutual funds and insurance. The study reveled that the decline has been due to very high net regulatory burden being imposed upon the entire banking system relative to that on the mutual funds and insurance companies. In India there is an urgent need to reduce the regulatory burden, particularly for banks vis-à-vis mutual funds and insurance companies, if the banks are expected to compete in free market place. (Mor, 1999)

Regulatory Requirements

The reference of regulatory requirements here are on the following issues-

Cash Reserve Ratio (CRR): From early 90's the monitory policy in India has been focusing on review of CRR. Off late RBI is concentrating more so on indirect instruments like Bank Rate and Open Market Operations, and felt that the CRR must be brought down to its minimum level of 3 percent at the earliest. It is also argued by some experts that instead of the complete Net Demand and Time Liabilities (NDTL) of banks, its application if restricted only to cash and cash like instruments, it would be more effective as an instrument of monetary policy and by applying the ratio, for the senior bonds that may be issued by banks to industry, is not in the interests of Monetary policy and this would further increase the cost of funds to the industry by almost at 1 percent.

Statutory Liquid Ratio (SLR): Though, the SLR has already reached its statutory minimum of 25 percent, some experts feel there is need to re-examine the present minimum limit, which is very high as per the international practices and could be brought down further by amending the Banking Regulation Act. Few banking experts extended to specific infrastructure projects as a part of SLR, since these facilities have directly replaced similar financing by Government of India.

Priority Sector: The whole issue of priority sector needs a closer look. The S.H Khan panel called for modifications in defining the priority sector by excluding all infrastructure loans from the net bank credit for the priority sector. It has also suggested the creation of an alternative mechanism to finance the priority sector.

Even the international experience of banks in Asia-Pacific region had a 'must serve' obligation towards priority sector and the result was discriminatory and inefficient performance without the support of commercial mindset.

Distinction between Maturity and Duration

This is the another issue of debate between long term and short term. Somehow DFIs are the suppliers of term finance, where the maturity is clearly specified which could be between 3 years to 7 years, where as banks are providers of short-term finance where in reality bank finance in a way amounts to financing in perpetuity since there are in general no definite maturity dates. Usually the deposit base of the banks have are short duration but with a variably high interest rates but its not the case with DFIs. Their funds have a longer duration with less interest rates.

The interim report of S H Khan committee has argued that the distinction between commercial and investment banking have become increasingly blurred with banks providing both working capital and term loans to corporates but DFIs can provide only term loans as they cannot accept short term deposits.

The committee further argued that DFIs should be given banking licenses eventually and until then they should be allowed to establish 100 percent banking subsidiaries while they continue to play their present role.

Optimal Transition Path

Viable transition path is one of the major areas of concern for institutions which are desirous of moving in the direction of universal banking. The transition path contains several operational and regulatory issues for information and guidance of DFIs. The S H Khan working group and the discussion paper on the subject prepared by RBI eventually felt that DFIs should transform themselves into commercial banks but in a phased manner.

The committee also recommended that DFIs can have 100 percent owned banking subsidiaries which would be extremely beneficial to them. If this happens, then it would allow DFIs to gain expertise in the area of commercial banking which would in turn help the DFIs if they are seriously looking at the prospect of converting into a commercial bank. Also the 100 percent subsidarisation allows banks to have a full access to capital base of DFIs and gain substantial knowledge in the area of project financing.

The RBI has asked FIs, which are interested to convert itself into a universal bank, to submit their plans for transition to a universal bank for consideration and further discussions. FIs need to formulate a road map for the transition path and strategy for smooth conversion into a universal bank over a specified time frame. The plan should specifically provide for full compliance with prudential norms as applicable to banks over the proposed period.

Considerations

Caution must be applied on Universal banking because of the following considerations:

1. Dis-intermediation (i.e replacement of traditional bank intermediation between savers and borrowers by a capital market process) is only a decade old in India and has badly slowed down due to loss of investors' confidence.
2. There is an ample room for financial deepening (by banks & DFIs) since loan market will continue to grow.
3. DFIs as a folder of equity in most of the projects promoted in the past have never used the tool advantageously.
4. DFIs are now only moving into working capital finance, an area in which they need to gain lot of expertise and this involves creation of network of services (including branches) in all fields like remittances, collections etc.
5. Reforms in the Indian capital market is still in the half way stage. The priority will be to ensure branch expansions, financial deepening of credit markets, and creation of an efficient credit delivery mechanism that can compete with the capital market.

Salient operational and regulatory issues to be addressed by the FIs for conversion into a Universal Bank [RBI circular]

Reserve Requirements

Compliance with the cash reserve ratio and statutory liquidity ratio requirements (under Section 42 of RBI Act, 1934, and Section 24 of the Banking Regulation Act, 1949, respectively) would be mandatory for an FI after its conversion into a universal bank.

Permissible Activities

Any activity of an FI currently undertaken but not permissible for a bank under Section 6(1) of the B. R. Act, 1949, may have to be stopped or divested after its conversion into a universal bank.

Disposal of Non-banking Assets

Any immovable property, howsoever acquired by an FI, would, after its conversion into a universal bank, be required to be disposed of within the maximum period of 7 years from the date of acquisition, in terms of Section 9 of the Banking Regulation Act.

Composition of the Board

Changing the composition of the Board of Directors might become necessary for some of the FIs after their conversion into a universal bank, to ensure compliance with the provisions of Section 10(A) of the B. R. Act, which requires at least 51% of the total number of directors to have special knowledge and experience.

Prohibition on Floating Charge of Assets

The floating charge, if created by an FI, over its assets, would require, after its conversion into a universal bank, ratification by the Reserve Bank of India under Section 14(A) of the Banking Regulation Act, since a banking company is not allowed to create-a floating charge on the undertaking or any property of the company unless duly certified by RBI as required under the Section.

Nature of Subsidiaries

If any of the existing subsidiaries of an FI is engaged in an activity not permitted under Section 6(1) of the B R Act, then on conversion of the FI into a universal bank, delinking of such subsidiary / activity from the operations of the universal bank would become necessary since Section 19 of the Act permits a bank to have subsidiaries only for one or more of the activities permitted under Section 6(1) of Banking Regulation Act.

Restriction on Investments

An FI with equity investment in companies in excess of 30 per cent of the paid up share capital of that company or 30 per cent of its own paid-up share capital and reserves, whichever is less, on its conversion into a universal bank, would need to divest such excess holdings to secure compliance with the provisions of Section 19(2) of the Banking Regulation Act, which prohibits a bank from holding shares in a company in excess of these limits.

Connccted Lending

Section 20 of the Banking Regulation Act prohibits grant of loans and advances by a bank on security of its own shares or grant of loans or advances on behalf of any of its directors or to any firm in which its director/manager or employee or guarantor is interested. The compliance with these provisions would be mandatory after conversion of an FI to a universal bank.

Licensing

An FI converting into a universal bank would be required to obtain a banking license from RBI under Section 22 of the Banking Regulation Act, for carrying on banking business in India, after complying with the applicable conditions.

Branch Network

An FI, after its conversion into a bank, would also be required to comply with extant branch licensing policy of RBI under which the new banks are required to allot at east 25 per cent of their total number of branches in semi-urban and rural areas.

Assets in India

An FI after its conversion into a universal bank, will be required to ensure that at the close of business on the last Friday of every quarter, its total assets held in India are not less than 75 per cent of its total demand and time liabilities in India, as required of a bank under Section 25 of the Banking Regulation Act.

Format of Annual Reports

After converting into a universal bank, an FI will be required to publish its annual balance sheet and profit and loss account in the in the forms set out in the Third Schedule to the B R Act, as prescribed for a banking company under Section 29 and Section 30 of the Banking Regulation Act.

Managerial Remuneration of the Chief Executive Officers

On conversion into a universal bank, the appointment and remuneration of the existing Chief Executive Officers may have to be reviewed with the approval of RBI in terms of the provisions of Section 35 B of the Banking Regulation

Act. The Section stipulates fixation of remuneration of the Chairman and Managing Director of a bank by Reserve Bank of India taking into account the profitability, net NPAs and other financial parameters. Under the Section, prior approval of RBI would also be required for appointment of Chairman and Managing Director.

Deposit Insurance

An FI, on conversion into a universal bank, would also be required to comply with the requirement of compulsory deposit insurance from DICGC up to a maximum of Rs.1 lakh per account, as applicable to the banks.

Authorized Dealer's License

Some of the FIs at present hold restricted AD license from RBI, Exchange Control Department to enable them to undertake transactions necessary for or incidental to their prescribed functions. On conversion into a universal bank, the new bank would normally be eligible for full-fledged authorized dealer license and would also attract the full rigour of the Exchange Control Regulations applicable to the banks at present, including prohibition on raising resources through external commercial borrowings.

Priority Sector Lending

On conversion of an FI to a universal bank, the obligation for lending to "priority sector" up to a prescribed percentage of their 'net bank credit' would also become applicable to it.

Prudential Norms

After conversion of an FI in to a bank, the extant prudential norms of RBI for the all-India financial institutions would no longer be applicable but the norms as applicable to banks would be attracted and will need to be fully complied with.

Concluding Remarks

The following are the steps suggested:

a. Equalise the net regulatory burden across the financial system (including banks, DFIs, mutual funds, NBFCs and Insurance companies).

b. Lower the regulatory burden on the over regulated entities.

c. Promote and encourage strong competition.

d. Do not allow the merger of a weak bank with a viably strong DFI or vice-versa.

e. DFIs should be permitted to set up a 100 percent owned banking subsidiaries.

f. Need is felt to re-examine the minimum level of SLR requirement in order to meet the best of international standards.

BIBLIOGRAPHY

Adams, T.F.M. : *A Financial History of the New Japan*, Kodansha International Ltd., Lokyo, 1972.

Ahluwalia, Montek S.: *"Reforming India's Financial Sector: An Overview"*, OUP, New Delhi, 1999.

Aliber, R. Z.: *The International Market for Foreign Exchange*, New York, Praeger, 1969.

Ariel Buira: *Challenges to the World Bank and IMF: Developing Country Perspectives*, London, Anthem Press, 2003.

Arrow, Kenneth J.: *Social Choice and Individual Values*, New York, Wiley, 1951.

Ashok, Vasant: *Indian Economy in the World Setting*, Bombay, Himalaya, 1988.

Auerbach, Alan J.: *Fiscal Policy, Lessons from Economic Research*, The MIT Press, Cambridge Massachusetts, London, 1997.

Bandow, Doug, and Ian Vasquez: *Perpetuating Poverty: The World Bank, the IMF, and the Developing World*, Washington, DC: Cato Institute, 1994.

Besley, T.: *How do Merket Failures Justify Interventions in Rural Credit Markets?*, Washington, D. C., World Bank, 1994

Bhagwati, J.: *Trade, Balance of Payments and Growth: Essays in Honor of C. P. Kindleberger*, Amsterdam, North-Holland Publishing Company, 1971.

Bhagwati, Jagdish: *India in Transition: Freeing the Economy*, Oxford, Clarendon Press, 1993.

Bhuleshkar, Vasant: *Indian Economy in the World Setting*, Bombay, Himalaya, 1988.

Bouman, F.J.A.: *Small, Short and Unsecured: Informal Rural Finance in India*, Delhi, Oxford University Press, 1989.

Campbell, J.Y., Lo, A.W.: *The Econometrics of Financial Markets*, Princeton University Press, 1996.

Chaudhuri, Pramit: *The Indian Economy: Poverty and Development*, New York, St. Martin's Press, 1979.

Connolly, M.: *The International Monetary System: Choices for the Future*, New York, Praeger, 1983.

Cooley, Thomas F.: *Frontiers of Business Cycle Research*, Princeton University Press, 1995.

Desai, Vasant: *A Study of Rural Economics: A Systems Approach*, Bombay, Himalaya, 1983.

Dhingra, C.: *The Indian Economy: Resources, Planning, Development, and Problems*, Delhi, Sultan Chand, 1983.

Dornbush, R.: *International Economic Policy*, Baltimore, The Johns Hopkins University Press, 1979.

Downs, Anthony: *An Economic Theory of Democracy*, New York, Harper and Row, 1957.

Edwards, S.: *Capital Controls, Exchange Rate and Monetary Policy in the World Economy*, Cambridge, Cambridge University Press, 1995.

Eleanor B. Steinberg and Joseph A. Yager: *New Means of Financing International Needs: Possible Sources of Finance*, Washington D.C.: The Brookings Institution, 1978.

Gerald, K.: *The Less Developed Countries in the International Economy*, Cambridge, Cambridge University Press, 1975.

Goldsmith, W.: *The Financial Development of India, 1860-1977*, New Haven, Yale University Press, 1983.

Greer, Douglas F.: *Industrial Organization and Public Policy*, MacMillan Publishing Company, 1992.

Guhan, S.: *The World Bank's Lending in South Asia*, Washington, Brookings Institution, 1995.

Hart, Oliver: *Firms, Contracts, and Financial Structure*, Clarendon Press, Oxford, 1995.

Hauft, Ottomar: *Distribution of Stock of Money*, Effingham, London, 1892.

Hinshaw, R.: *Global Economic Priorities: The Hamburg Dialogue*, Hamburg, Verlag Weltarchiv, 1983.

Hoshii, Iwao: *A Financial History of the New Japan*, Kodansha International Ltd., Lokyo, 1972.

Huang, Chi-fu: *Foundations of Financial Economics*, Prentice-Hall, 1988.

Jha, P.R.: *Agriculture and Economic Development*, New Delhi, Ashish, 1988.

Johnson, H.: *The Economics of Common Currencies*, London, George Allen & Unwin Ltd., 1973.

Le Prestre, Philippe: *The World Bank and the Environmental Challenge*, London, Associated University Presses, 1989.

MacKinley, A.C.: *The Econometrics of Financial Markets*, Princeton University Press, 1996.

Magliveras, Konstantinos D. *Banks, Fraud and Crime*, Lloyd's of London Press, London, 2000.

McCallum, J. : *Global Disequilibrium*, London, MacMillan, 1992.

McLellan, Elisabeth P.: *The International Monetary Fund: Overview, Issues and Bibliography*, Happague, NY: Nova Publishers, 2002.

Michael Connolly, *The International Monetary System: Choices for the Future*, New York, Praeger, 1983.

Musalem, Errico, Luca & Alberto: *Offshore Banking: An Analysis of Micro-and Macro-Prudential Issues*, IMF, Washington, D.C., 1999.

Ottomar, H.: *Distribution of Stock of Money*, Effingham, London, 1892.

Paul, Kegan : *Money and the Mechanism of Exchange,* Oxford, London, 1890.

Peet, Richard, Born, Beate: *Unholy Trinity: The IMF, World Bank, and WTO*, New York, Zed Books, 2003.

Pettifor, Ann: *Real World Economic Outlook: The Legacy of Globalization: Debt and Deflation*, New York, Palgrave MacMillan, 2003.

Polak, J.J. : *The New International Monetary System*, New York, Columbia University Press, 1978.

Raj, K.N.: *New Economic Policy*, Delhi, Oxford University Press, 1986.

Ranade, Sudhanshu: *Rural Banking Adrift*, Bombay, Jaico Publishing House, 1984.

Rao, M.G. and R.J. Chelliah: *Survey of Research in Indian Fiscal Federalism*, National Institute of Public Finance and Policy, New Delhi, 1991.

Robert Z. Aliber: *The International Market for Foreign Exchange*, New York, Praeger, 1969.

Savla, Sandeep: *Money Laundering and Financial Intermediaries*, The Hague and Boston, Kluwer Law International, 2001.

Sebastian Edwards: *Capital Controls, Exchange Rate and Monetary Policy in the World Economy,* Cambridge, Cambridge University Press, 1995.

Seligman, E. R. A. : *Currency Inflation and Public Debts,* New York, 1922.

Sinha, R.K.: *Economic Development since Independence*, New Delhi, Deep and Deep, 1988.

Vines, David and Christopher Gilbert: *The IMF and its Critics: Reform of the Global Financial Architecture*, Cambridge, Cambridge University Press, 2004.

Wolfe, J.N.: *Value, Capital and Growth*, Chicago, Edinburgh University Press. 1968.

INDEX

J

L

M

❑❑❑